ICED CHRISTMAS CAKE

PLAN AND COOK

by

G. COCKER & B. V. GODFREY

*Lecturers in Housecraft : Gloucestershire Training
College of Domestic Science*

*With a coloured frontispiece, 8 photographs,
and 10 line drawings*

J. M. DENT & SONS LTD
10–13 BEDFORD ST, LONDON, W.C.2

All rights reserved
Made in Great Britain
at the
Aldine Press · Letchworth · Herts
for
J. M. DENT & SONS LTD
Aldine House · Bedford Street · London
First published 1954
Last reprinted 1963

CONTENTS

CONTENTS

ILLUSTRATIONS

(Photographs by H. Walwin, A.R.P.S., Gloucester)

I
PLANNING EVERYDAY MEALS

Meals

THE day's meals vary considerably with different circumstances and to some extent in the north and south of the country. The following variations occur:

(a) Breakfast.
    Lunch.
    Afternoon tea.
    Dinner.

(b) Breakfast.
    Dinner.
    Afternoon tea.
    Supper.

(c) Breakfast.
    Dinner.
    High tea.
    Bedtime snack.

(a) In this case the main meal of the day is served in the evening at 7 p.m. or thereabouts. The midday meal is a lighter one. Tea consists of tea to drink with very little to eat, perhaps dainty sandwiches, or scones with jam and cakes. This would be served at 4–4.30 p.m.

(b) In the second case the main meal is at midday, followed by a light tea as before. Supper at 7–8 p.m. would consist of an easily prepared meal, often including dishes assembled during the morning's cooking which, with little effort, may be heated or served at supper-time.

(c) In the third instance the main meal is at midday, followed by a cup of tea only at 4 p.m., and a substantial tea known as high tea at 5.30–6 p.m. High tea usually consists of a cooked savoury dish served with bread and butter, followed by bread and butter and jam or scones and jam and cakes. Instead of a variety of cakes a fruit flan or some kind of tart is sometimes served, or stewed fruit with cream or custard and suitable biscuits.

Examples of suitable menus for these meals follow, together with recipes for some of the dishes mentioned. The quantities suggested are for an average family of four. The general rules for meal planning must be considered and modifications made where necessary.

Rules for meal planning.

1. Think of the nutritive value of the meals for the whole day, including foods from each of the three main groups— Body Builders, Body Protectors, Energy Givers. (See *Look and Cook*, 'Right Feeding for Health,' p. 8.)

2. Think of the ages, sex, and occupations of the family.

3. Think of the cost of the food, planning to include home-grown produce and foods in season. Also consider the food to use up from the larder.

4. Think of fuel economy, making good use of the cooker when it is hot, or planning to make the whole meal on the top of the stove or to use a steamer or pressure cooker to the best advantage.

5. Think of the housewife's other duties, making meals which may be sensibly prepared in relation to the rest of her work.

6. Think of the time of the year, planning suitably for hot and cold days.

7. Think of the foods in relation to each other so that 'bite' is given, avoiding serving all soft foods, and also avoiding repetition of type, colour, flavour, etc.

Breakfasts

Breakfast is the first meal of the day, and it is important for everyone to have as good a breakfast as possible.

Special points.

1. Allow plenty of time for eating breakfast.
2. If necessary the table may be laid the night before.
3. Vary the menu.
4. Always try to include a little food from the body-building group.
5. A good breakfast should consist of two or three courses, and a hot drink.

Choose from among the following suggestions, but remember that there are many other dishes that are also suitable for breakfast.

To begin	*The main part*
Porridge	Bacon and fried egg
Cereals	Bacon and tomato
Grape-fruit	Bacon and sausage
Stewed apples, figs,	Bacon and fried bread
prunes, or rhubard	Egg and Marmite toast
Orange juice	Eggs—boiled, poached, scrambled
Tomato juice	Fish—kippers, herrings, haddock, fish cakes
	Potato cakes. Fried-up potatoes
	A selection of left-over mixtures served on buttered toast

To finish.

1. Bread or toast with dripping and Marmite.
2. Bread and butter, especially wholemeal or brown bread with Marmite, marmalade, honey, or syrup.
3. Toast with butter and marmalade, syrup, honey, or Marmite.

To drink.

Tea, coffee, cocoa, or chocolate.

To begin Breakfast

PORRIDGE

1. Serve porridge on very cold days. It should be hot, smooth, and of a creamy consistency.
2. Porridge made from oatmeal:
   This is very good but it must have plenty of time to cook thoroughly, at least 30 minutes. This porridge can often be cooked the night before.
3. Porridge made from rolled oats:
   These are sold in packets, and the instructions on the packet should be followed carefully. This kind of porridge takes about 10–15 minutes to cook.
4. Serve porridge in a soup plate or small deep dish. Serve with hot or cold milk, salt or sugar or syrup. Children often like soft brown sugar on their porridge.
5. Allow about ¼ pint porridge to each person.
6. Porridge burns easily; use a double cooker or have an asbestos mat under the pan. Do not attempt to hurry the cooking of porridge.

OATMEAL PORRIDGE

1½ pt. water.
¼–1 teasp. salt, according to taste.
3 oz. medium oatmeal.

To make.

1. Put the water and salt into a 2-pint pan. Bring to the boil.
2. Measure the oatmeal on to a piece of paper.
3. When the water is just boiling sift in the oatmeal slowly, stirring with a wooden spoon.
4. Stir until the porridge boils, then reduce the heat and leave to simmer very slowly for 30–45 minutes. Stir occasionally.
5. When ready taste and serve as described above.
6. Put the pan to soak at once.

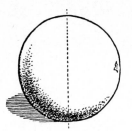

1. Cut across in half   2. Loosen each section

TO PREPARE A GRAPE-FRUIT

GRAPE-FRUIT

Grape-fruit makes a refreshing beginning to breakfast.

1. Grape-fruit is especially valuable for its vitamin C content, and therefore must not be prepared too soon before it is eaten.

2. Serve sprinkled with a little castor sugar.

3. If necessary, two grape-fruit can be made to serve five people by turning the sections out of their skins into fruit dishes and dividing the sections and juice into the desired number of portions. Canned grape-fruit is also served in this way.

To prepare grape-fruit.

1. Rub over the skin of the grape-fruit with a damp cloth.

2. Roll well until it is a good round shape.

3. Using a stainless knife cut across in half, then stand it on a plate to avoid losing any juice.

4. With a special grape-fruit knife or a stainless vegetable knife loosen round the grape-fruit between the fruit and the skin. Be careful not to cut into the white pith which is very bitter.

5. Loosen each section of grape-fruit by sliding the knife

from centre to outside each side of every piece of dividing skin.

6. Sprinkle with 1 teaspoonful of castor sugar.
7. Serve in an individual fruit dish or on a small plate.

STEWED FRUIT

Stewed fruit alone or with cereals makes a very good beginning to breakfast.

1. Apples, figs, prunes, and early rhubarb are the most popular breakfast fruits.
2. Serve with sugar if necessary. No custard is served with fruit at breakfast; cream or milk may be served if liked.
3. The fruit is stewed in the usual way. (See *Look and Cook*, p. 29.)
4. Fruit for breakfast could be stewed in a cooling oven the day before.

ORANGE OR TOMATO JUICE

Many people like canned fruit juice or tomato juice for breakfast.

Orange juice is best made from fresh oranges squeezed and poured into small glasses. Sweeten to taste.

Serve ½–1 orange to each person.

CEREALS

There is a great variety of cereals available for breakfast.

1. Store the packet in a dry place to keep the cereal fresh and crisp.
2. Vary the kind of cereal occasionally.
3. Serve in a small fruit dish with hot or cold milk and sugar.
4. Allow people to help themselves to milk as the cereal soon becomes soft if the milk is poured over too soon.

The Main Part

BACON AND EGGS FOR FOUR

2–4 rashers bacon.
4 eggs.
A little lard or dripping for frying the eggs.

To cook.

1. Put a serving dish to warm.
2. Use a pair of kitchen scissors to trim off the rinds of the bacon. Cut the rashers into lengths to fit the frying-pan; remember that bacon shrinks when cooked.
3. Put the bacon in the frying-pan and fry slowly until the fat has changed colour and the bacon is becoming crisp. This takes 3–5 minutes.
4. Using a fork, lift out the bacon and keep it hot on the serving dish.
5. The fat from the bacon should be enough to fry the eggs. If necessary a little dripping or lard may be added and allowed to become hot, or the bacon fat may be poured over the bacon and lard used for frying the eggs.
6. Break the eggs one at a time into a cup or saucer. Test for freshness.
7. The fat should just cover the bottom of the pan; it must be hot, but not smoking. Slide the eggs one at a time into the fat. All four eggs may be fried at once, but they should lie flat. In a small pan fry two at a time.
8. Cook over gentle heat, basting the eggs with the fat until the white is firm.
9. Use a fish slice or palette knife to loosen the eggs and lift carefully on to the hot serving dish. Serve at once.

FRIED TOMATOES

These make a change and can be served with fried bacon,
sausages, or on a slice of fried bread.

> Allow 1–2 tomatoes for each person.
> Fat for frying.

To cook.

1. Wipe the tomatoes with a clean damp cloth.
2. Cut the tomatoes in two.
3. Heat a little dripping, bacon fat, or lard in a frying-pan
   until it is hot, but not quite smoking.
4. Put the tomatoes in, cut sides up. Tomatoes sizzle and
   splash, so avoid frying quickly.
5. Cook until almost tender, then turn over to finish cooking.
6. Tomatoes take about 5 minutes to cook, and should be soft,
   slightly brown on top but still quite whole.
7. Lift out and serve at once with the cut sides up.

FRIED BREAD

This is useful for serving with bacon.

> Allow $\frac{1}{2}$–1 slice of bread to each person.
> Bacon fat or dripping for frying.

To cook.

1. Cut the bread $\frac{1}{4}$ inch thick; stale bread is good for frying.
2. Make the fat hot.   Dip both sides of the bread in the fat and
   then leave to fry until crisp and golden brown, turning
   when one side is ready.
3. Lift out and serve at once.

EGG AND MARMITE TOAST FOR FOUR

This makes an economical and nutritious breakfast. The
Marmite may be omitted if desired.

1 egg.	4 slices of bread.
6 tablesp. milk.	A little Marmite.
Salt and pepper.	Fat for frying.

To make.

1. Break the egg into a basin, beat well and add the milk and seasoning.
2. Pour the egg mixture on to a large meat dish.
3. Spread a little Marmite on both sides of the slices of bread.
4. Soak the bread in the egg mixture. Allow 15–20 minutes for this, but it is better if it can be covered and left soaking overnight.
5. Heat enough fat to cover the bottom of the frying-pan; when it is hot put in 1 or 2 slices of the soaked bread and fry on both sides until it is golden brown. Repeat with the rest of the bread.
6. When ready lift on to a hot dish and serve at once.

Note.

The bread will be soft and should be lifted carefully. After cooking, the bread, although golden brown, remains soft and is similar in texture to a pancake.

SAVOURY LEFT-OVERS

An interesting change for breakfast can be made from any savoury left-overs, e.g. smoked haddock, sardines, baked beans, fried liver.

To prepare.

1. Make a thick slice of toast, butter it and keep it hot.
2. Mince or chop the mixture if necessary. Warm very thoroughly in a saucepan with a little margarine or left-over sauce or gravy.
3. When thoroughly hot, season, and pile on the hot buttered toast. Serve at once.
4. Fried bread may be used instead of toast.

Refer to *Look and Cook* for cooking eggs, kippers, herrings, fish cakes, and sausages.

To finish Breakfast

1. Most people like to finish breakfast with 1 or 2 slices of toast or bread and butter.

2. Make the toast before beginning breakfast, and stand it in a toast rack.

3. Serve butter in a butter dish and marmalade in a jam or marmalade pot. Honey is usually left in its own jar, but make sure the outside of the jar is kept clean.

4. *Dripping :* Dripping from the meat, or made from pieces of fat cut from the meat and rendered down, is delicious for breakfast. Pork and beef dripping are especially good.

   If the dripping has very little sediment use a little Marmite to give it flavour.

   Some people like to sprinkle a little salt over the dripping.

A Hot Drink for Breakfast

Tea or coffee are both popular breakfast drinks.
Cocoa makes a sustaining drink, particularly for children.

TEA

$\frac{1}{2}$–1 teasp. tea to each person, and 1 teasp. extra for the pot.
Boiling water.

To make.

1. Fill the kettle with freshly drawn cold water. Put it on to boil.

2. Stand the teapot and hot-water jug on the table.

3. When the kettle is boiling pour a little water into the teapot and hot-water jug to make them thoroughly warm.

4. Throw away the water and measure the tea into the pot.

5. Pour the boiling water over the tea. Fill the teapot about

three-quarters full.   Fill the hot-water jug with boiling
water.

6. Allow the tea to stand 3 minutes before pouring out.   Use a
   tea-cosy to keep the tea hot and stand the teapot and
   hot-water jug on a stand or mat.   Remember to have a
   jug of cold milk and sugar on the table.

COFFEE

Coffee should be fresh.   Do not buy large quantities at a
time.   Keep it in an air-tight tin.

For breakfast for four people make $1\frac{1}{2}$ pints coffee.

> 3 heaped tablesp. coffee. $1\frac{1}{2}$ pt. boiling water.
> 1–$1\frac{1}{2}$ pt. milk.

To make.

1. Fill a kettle with 2 pints of freshly drawn cold water and
   put it on to boil.
2. When the water is boiling pour a little into an earthenware
   jug or coffee-pot to warm it, then empty it away.
3. Measure the coffee into the warmed pot.
4. Pour the boiling water over the coffee.
5. Use a tablespoon and stir thoroughly.
6. Cover with a lid and leave to stand in a warm place for 10
   minutes, e.g. on the side of the stove.
7. Heat an equal quantity of milk.   Do not boil the milk.
   When hot, strain carefully into another warmed coffee-
   pot or jug so that the milk and coffee may be mixed to
   suit each person.

Note.

Any coffee left from breakfast should be strained ready to warm up in a
pan for elevenses.

COCOA

For four people allow:

> 6 teasp. cocoa.   6 teasp. sugar.
> 2 pt. milk and water mixed.

To make.

1. Measure the cocoa and sugar into a wide-necked jug.
2. Warm the milk and water, and when just warm pour a little over the cocoa.
3. Blend the cocoa and warm liquid to a smooth cream, using a wooden spoon.
4. Add the blended cocoa to the rest of the liquid and return to the heat. Stir until boiling and boil for 2–3 minutes.
5. Serve in the jug used for mixing; rinse this if necessary and keep it warm until the cocoa is ready.

Note.

1. Some people prefer to add their own sugar at the table.
2. Cocoa may be made with water. Cold milk may then be added as desired.

MORNING COFFEE FOR THE VISITOR

Elevenses

TRAY LAYING

When laying a tray always think of the following things:

1. Have a clean polished tray.
2. If using a cloth it must fit the tray and be clean and quite flat.

3. Use mats for hot jugs.
4. Use the prettiest china available and place the things neatly and in the best position for convenient use (see photograph, p. 14).
5. When carrying a tray always carry carefully, holding the heaviest side towards you.

Lunches and Dinners

1. Dinner is usually the main meal of the day, and should be a substantial, well-balanced meal.
2. Lunch is a lighter form of dinner. This is usually served at home when some members of the family only get a light meal at their work, and the whole family have a substantial high tea or supper when they return home.
3. A dinner should consist of two courses: the main dish, potatoes and a vegetable, followed by a pudding. Gravy and sauces should be included according to the dish.
4. If the servings are small, or to make a change, the meal can be made into three courses by serving soup at the beginning.
5. Cheese and biscuits are sometimes served instead of a pudding or after the pudding, especially for a lunch.
6. When preparing a dinner, plan the whole meal carefully so that everything is ready at the right moment. Allow time for making the sauce or gravy and try to have the pudding dished and kept hot before starting the meal.
7. Remember to allow different cooking times for different vegetables: e.g. swedes and carrots need 40 minutes, Brussels sprouts only 10 minutes.
8. Lay the table in good time before you become busy with the dishing-up.

Choosing the Meal

Read the introduction to this section of the book carefully for rules and special points.

It is particularly important when planning dinners to choose the dishes carefully to fit in with the rest of your work. For example, on busy cleaning- or washing-days choose dishes which will need very little attention, e.g. hot-pot, rice pudding.

Suggestions for lunches and dinners.

Recipes and methods for dishes marked * will be found in *Look and Cook*.

Remember that many of the dishes for high tea and supper are also suitable for lunch and dinner.

Soup	Main Course
* Mixed vegetable.	* Roast meat.
* Lentil.	Braised meat.
Tomato.	* Fried or grilled chops or steak.
Scotch broth.	Mixed grill.
	* Stews—hot-pot, brown stew.
Vegetables	* Shepherd's pie.
* Potatoes:	Baked stuffed liver.
Boiled, mashed,	Stuffed marrow.
fried, baked, roast,	Curried meat.
sauté.	Russian fish pie.
* Carrots. * Swedes.	* Baked stuffed fillets fish.
* Parsnips.	Fish croquettes.
* Cabbage. * Sprouts.	* Fried coated fish.
* Cauliflower.	Fried fish in yeast batter.
Leeks. Celery.	* Macaroni cheese.
Marrow.	* Cheese pudding.
Tomatoes.	Cheese eggs.

Puddings

* Fruit pie.   * Jam tart.
* Steamed suet puddings.
* Steamed cake mixture puddings.
  Steamed ground rice pudding.
    Queen of puddings.
* Pancakes.   Apple fritters.
* Milk puddings.   * Stewed fruit.
  Fruit fool.   * Fruit salad.
* Baked cake mixtures.
* Apple charlotte.   Apple crackle.
  Baked apples.

Sauces

* Gravy.
* White blended sauce.
* White roux sauce.
  Tomato sauce.
  Brown roux sauce.
* Custard sauce.
* Jam or syrup sauce.
  Egg custard sauce.
  Economical egg custard.

Soups

Soup makes a welcome addition to dinner on a cold day or when some good stock is available.

TOMATO SOUP FOR FOUR

1 lb. fresh, canned, or bottled tomatoes.
1 carrot.   1 onion.   1 stick celery.
1 oz. margarine or dripping.
A few bacon rinds.

2 pt. stock or 2 pt. water and a bone.
Salt. Pepper. $\frac{1}{2}$ teasp. sugar.
A blade of mace. $\frac{1}{2}$ a bay leaf.
1 oz. flour.

Note.

A little less stock is needed for canned or bottled tomatoes.

To make.

1. Prepare and slice the vegetables. Collect the other ingredients.   Keep the tomatoes separate.
2. Melt the margarine and add the bacon rinds.   Use a large pan—3–4 pint size.
3. Add the sliced vegetables and sauté or toss in the hot fat for a few minutes.   This makes the vegetables tasty, but

they should not be allowed to brown as this discolours the soup.

4. Add the sliced tomatoes, seasoning, herbs, stock. Cover with a lid, bring to the boil, and then reduce the heat and allow the soup to simmer slowly. The soup should simmer at least an hour to develop a good flavour.

5. When the vegetables are tender strain the soup into a basin. Press the soft pulpy part of the soup through the strainer or sieve. The herbs, bacon rinds, tomato seeds and skins, and the bone will be left.

6. Blend the flour with very little cold water until it is a smooth cream. This may be prepared while the soup is cooking.

7. Add the blended flour to the soup. Rinse the pan and pour the soup back.

8. Use a wooden spoon and stir the soup over the heat until it boils. Allow it to boil for 3 minutes to cook the flour.

9. Taste the soup, add more seasoning if necessary. The soup should be a creamy consistency. Add more stock or water, and reheat if too thick. Add more blended flour, off the heat, and re-boil if it is too thin.

10. Serve in a hot soup tureen or in warmed individual soup plates. Do not serve the soup until the family is ready for the meal.

11. Slices of bread, toast or fried dice of bread called croûtons are served with soup.

SCOTCH BROTH

A really good Scotch broth may be served as the main part of a dinner. It is a good way of using the cheaper cuts of meat to make a satisfying meal.

Allow 3–4 hours for cooking. It may be partly cooked the

day before. Cooking time may be shortened by using a pressure cooker.

1½ lb. scrag end neck of mutton or brisket of beef.	1 carrot.
	1 onion.
3–4 pt. cold water.	½ turnip.
2 oz. pearl barley.	Selection of other vegetables if
Salt and pepper.	available. Leek, celery, shredded cabbage. Peas.

To make.

1. Wash the barley in a strainer. Wipe the meat, remove excess fat, and cut up into small pieces.
2. Put the meat, barley, cold water, and salt into a large pan and put on to boil.
3. Prepare the vegetables and cut up into dice.
4. When the meat is boiling, skim with a metal spoon, add the vegetables and pepper, reduce the heat until the broth is just simmering.
5. Simmer the broth slowly for 3½ hours.
6. Remove surplus fat, or leave to get cold before removing and then skim off as for stock.
7. Reheat, taste, season, add the chopped parsley, and serve. The meat from the larger bones should be loosened into the broth and the bones removed. Broth is served in warmed soup plates.

BRAISED MEAT

Braising is a method of cooking that combines roasting with steaming. Braised meat has a delicious flavour. The method is suitable for lean pieces of meat that are not quite tender enough to roast.

Allow 30–40 minutes to the 1 lb. and 30 minutes over.

A bouquet garni is used for flavouring braised meat and some stews, soups, and sauces. This consists of a selection of spices and herbs tied loosely together in a small square of muslin. This little bag is cooked in the liquid with the other ingredients, but is removed before serving.

Select from among the following suggestions:

Blade of mace.
½ a bay leaf.
Peppercorns.

A small bunch of parsley.
A few sprigs of thyme or marjoram (use a a good pinch if the herbs are dried).

TO BRAISE A SMALL JOINT OF MEAT

2 lb. brisket of beef, or 2 lb. fillet of mutton or mutton chops or steak.
1 oz. dripping.
1 onion.
1 carrot.

½ turnip.
Small piece of celery.
Salt and pepper.
Bouquet garni.
1 pt. hot stock or water.
1 oz flour.

To cook.

1. Wipe the meat and tie into a firm joint if necessary.
2. Melt the dripping. When it is hot put in the meat and brown both sides.
3. While the meat is frying prepare the vegetables and cut into slices.
4. Lift out the meat on to a plate, using two spoons.
5. Put the sliced vegetables into the dripping and sauté slowly for about 10 minutes.
6. Prepare the herbs. Grease a circle of paper to fit the pan and make the stock or water hot.
7. Put the meat back on top of the bed of vegetables. Add the seasoning and herbs. Pour over the hot stock or water, which should just cover the vegetables but not the meat.
8. Cover the meat with the greased paper and put the lid on the pan.
9. Leave to simmer slowly for about 2 hours. Braising may be done on top or in a moderate oven. When braising in the oven choose a casserole type of pan with two short metal handles, and remember to use an oven-cloth whenever handling the pan. Brown paper may also be tied round the handles as a reminder.

10. When the meat is tender serve on a hot dish. The vegetables used for braising may be used for serving with the braise or sieved into the stock for making the gravy. Remember to remove the bouquet garni. A garnish of freshly boiled diced vegetables may be served round the braise in small heaps.

11. Blend the flour with a little cold water, add to the stock remaining in the pan, boil and add gravy-browning if necessary. Taste, season, and either pour the gravy round the braise or serve separately in a gravy-boat.

MIXED GRILL

This makes an attractive, quickly prepared dish for dinner. Choose a selection from the following to make sufficient for four people.

Lean, tender steak.	Sausages.	Watercress to
Mutton chops.	Sheep's kidney.	garnish.
2–4 tomatoes.	Bacon.	

Small chips may also be served with a mixed grill.

To cook.

1. Prepare the meat. Wipe and trim steak and chops. Steak is cooked in one piece and cut up after cooking. Prick the sausages. Trim off the rind of bacon. Cut round the circumference of the kidneys, open out and snip out the white core with a pair of scissors and then wash well. Keep the kidney in one piece. Cut the tomatoes across in two.

2. Heat the grill until it is red hot. Melt some dripping or lard, brush over the meat and the grid stand.

3. Put the tomatoes cut side up in the bottom of the grill pan. Arrange the meat on the grid and stand it in the pan over the tomatoes.

4. Cook quickly until both sides of the meat are brown. Use two spoons for turning. Reduce the heat and allow

about 10 minutes for the meat to cook through, turning from time to time. Thick pieces take longer than thin ones.

5. Serve on a hot meat-dish. Arrange the tomatoes round the meat, pour over the gravy from the grill pan, and garnish with a few bunches of well-washed watercress.

Note.

1. To turn the meat during braising or grilling use blunt utensils, as it is important not to penetrate the coating of the meat.

2. If chips are to be served, prepare everything beforehand. When the grill is almost ready reduce the heat so that it keeps hot without attention, and then fry the chips.

BAKED STUFFED LIVER

¾ lb. liver.
A few scraps of bacon.
¼ pt. water.

Stuffing: 3 tablesp. breadcrumbs.
2 teasp. chopped parsley.
Pinch of dried or fresh thyme.
1 oz. suet or margarine.
A little grated lemon rind if available.
Salt and pepper. Milk to bind.

To make.

1. Prepare a moderate oven.

2. Make the stuffing. Make the breadcrumbs; light coloured crusts may be used by cutting up finely. Add the chopped parsley, thyme, lemon rind, suet or margarine cut up into pieces, salt and pepper. Mix with a fork to a crumbly consistency that will just hold together. Beaten egg, milk, or stock are used for mixing.

3. Wash the liver and cut into flat slices. Allow one or two pieces for each person.

4. Place the liver in a Yorkshire-pudding tin. Cover each slice with stuffing, and put a small piece of bacon over the stuffing.

5. Pour the water round the liver and cover with a greased paper or a lid. The water should come three-quarters of the way up the liver.

6. Bake in a moderate oven for about 1 hour.

7. Test the liver to see if it is tender. Lift the slices on to a hot meat dish and keep them warm.

8. Blend the flour with a little cold water. Add to the gravy
   in the baking-tin, and stir over the heat to make a small
   quantity of good gravy. If the water has boiled away
   add a little more; the juices from the liver should make a
   well-flavoured gravy that does not need extra flavouring.
   Taste, season, and pour round the liver. Garnish with
   parsley.

Note.

1. This is a good way of cooking liver that is not very tender.
2. Frozen liver should be thawed out slowly on a plate over hot water
   before being sliced.

STUFFED MARROW

1 small, or half a large marrow.	*Stuffing :* $\frac{1}{2}$ lb. minced cooked meat.
2 tablesp. dripping for baking.	$\frac{1}{2}$ oz. dripping. $\frac{1}{2}$ oz. flour.
	$\frac{1}{4}$ pt. stock or water.
	Salt and pepper.
	Pinch of thyme. 2 teasp.
	chopped parsley. 1 onion.
	Other flavourings : Tomato, bacon, cooked
	vegetables.

To cook.

1. Peel and boil the onion if not already cooked.
2. Wash and peel the marrow. Take the peel off in thin
   lengths. A young marrow should peel easily. A
   marrow that has been kept or has grown very slowly has
   a very hard peel.   It is best to steam this kind of marrow
   for 1 hour before peeling and stuffing.
3. Cut one end off the peeled marrow and scoop out the
   seeds. Another way is to cut the marrow through
   lengthways into two pieces, remove the seeds, and tie
   together after stuffing.

To prepare the stuffing.

4. Melt $\frac{1}{2}$ oz. dripping, add the flour, mix together, then add
   the stock or water to make a thick gravy. A little browning or half a meat cube may be added if liked.
5. Add the minced meat, chopped onion, parsley, thyme,

B

seasoning, and any flavourings available to the gravy. These may be mixed together in the pan or in a basin; the mixture should be moist.

6. Put the 2 tablespoonfuls dripping into a baking-tin large enough to take the marrow and put it into the oven to get hot.

7. Put the stuffing into the prepared marrow. Tie the end on, or tie the two halves together. Use a clean, fine, white string for cooking.

8. Lift out the hot dripping, put the marrow into the tin, baste with the dripping, and cover with a greased paper.

9. Bake in a fairly hot oven for about 1 hour. Very large marrows may take longer. A marrow which has already been partly cooked before peeling will take about 40 minutes.

10. When the marrow is tender, serve on a hot meat dish with the liquor from the tin poured over.

Note.

1. Left-over gravy may be used for mixing and serving if available.
2. Fresh minced meat may also be used, but it should be cooked in the gravy for about 10 minutes before being mixed with the rest of the stuffing.

BROWN SAUCE

A good brown sauce or gravy can be made by making a brown roux, and then adding stock or water. This kind of sauce can be used wherever a gravy thickened by blending has been mentioned, e.g. with roast meat, brown stew, shepherd's pie, rissoles, for moistening the stuffing and serving with stuffed liver or marrow.

This sauce takes longer to make than a blended sauce, but once the method is fully understood and memorized it is quite simple and a richer flavour can be obtained.

1 oz. dripping.	½ onion.	½ turnip.	Piece celery.
1 oz flour.	1 carrot.	Bacon rind.	Pepper.
½ to 1 pt. stock.	Bouquet garni.	Salt.	

The amount of stock varies according to the consistency required.

To make.

1. Peel the vegetables and cut up into small pieces. Keep the root vegetables in a small basin of water.
2. Melt the dripping, add the flour; stir in carefully, using a metal spoon. Spread over the bottom of the pan and cook over gentle heat until the flour is chestnut-coloured. Stir the flour so that it browns evenly. This will take about 7 minutes.
3. Remove from the heat, and add the stock slowly. Be careful of the steam made when the stock is first added. Stir until a smooth sauce is obtained.
4. Add the vegetables, bouquet garni, and seasoning. Bring to the boil, then simmer gently for 40 minutes or until the vegetables are tender.
5. Strain the sauce through a gravy-strainer into a basin, rub the soft parts of the vegetables through the strainer. Taste and re-season if necessary.
6. Use as required.

Reheat the sauce and adjust the consistency for serving as a separate sauce. Use cold and thick for mixing with cooked meat or stuffing.

When using a brown sauce for stews the vegetables are omitted as they form part of the ingredients of the stew. The brown sauce is made first and the meat and vegetables added after. In this case the chopped onion is usually fried in the dripping to give a good flavour; it is then lifted out, the flour added, and browned, and then the onions added again with the stock.

CURRY OF COLD MEAT

½ lb. cold cooked meat.	1 apple.
½ oz. dripping.	1 oz. sultanas.
½ onion.	1 dessertsp. chutney.
½ oz. flour.	1 teasp. jam.
1–2 tablesp. curry-powder.	½ teasp. salt.
½ pt. stock or water.	A squeeze of lemon juice.

To make.

1. Peel and chop the onion and apple.
2. Melt the dripping, add the chopped onion, and fry until it is golden brown.
3. Add the flour and curry-powder, stir in using an old wooden spoon, and fry slowly together for 3 minutes.
4. Add the stock and make a thick sauce. Add the chopped apple, washed sultanas, chutney, jam, lemon juice, and salt. Stir together and cook very slowly for 30 minutes, stirring occasionally. Add a little more stock if necessary.
5. Cut the cold meat into neat chunky pieces. It may be minced if liked.
6. Add the meat to the curry in time to warm through very thoroughly before serving. The meat must not be allowed to boil, only to reheat.
7. Taste, season if necessary, and serve on a hot, deep dish.

Note.

Boiled rice is usually served with curry. Mashed potatoes or macaroni can also be served. These are made into a border round the curry and garnished with chopped parsley.

TO BOIL RICE FOR CURRY

3 oz. rice.

To cook.

1. Prepare a pan of boiling salted water.
2. Wash the rice in a strainer.
3. Put the rice into the boiling water and cook quickly for 15 minutes, or until the rice is just tender.
4. Strain the rice and wash once more under the running cold tap. This allows the grains to separate.
5. Turn on to a greased meat dish. Cover with greased paper and leave in a warm place to dry for about 1 hour. Separate the grains occasionally with a fork.
6. When serving with curry the rice should be boiled as soon as the curry sauce has been made; this allows time for drying.

RUSSIAN FISH PIE

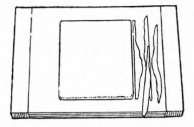

1. Pastry rolled to 8-in. square, trimmed lightly to straighten.

2. Pastry arranged on a baking-tray with the fish mixture in the centre.

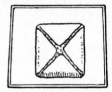

3. The corners folded to the centre and the joins flaked to seal.

4. The leaves arranged between the sealed edges.

To shape a Russian Fish Pie

6 oz. rough puff or flaky pastry.
¾ lb. white fish—cod, hake, or fresh haddock.
1 teasp. chopped parsley.

½ oz. margarine.
½ oz. flour.
¼ pt. fish liquor or milk.
Salt and pepper.

To make.

1. Prepare a fairly hot oven.
2. Wash and trim the fish, put into a fireproof dish or a baking-tin, pour over sufficient milk or milk and water to cover the bottom of the tin.
3. Put the fish in the oven and allow to cook until it is white and will lift easily from the bone. This will take about 20–30 minutes.
4. Make the pastry and leave to stand in a cool place. (*Look and Cook*, pp. 109 and 112.)

5. Chop the parsley. Melt the margarine, add the flour, and make a roux for the sauce. (Refer to *Look and Cook* for sauces.)

6. When the fish is ready measure the liquor from the tin, make up to ¼ pint with milk, and use for making the sauce.

7. Turn the oven up to very hot.

8. Lift the fish on to a plate, remove the skin and bones, and flake the fish with a fork. Add the parsley, 2 tablespoonfuls sauce, and salt and pepper.

9. Roll the pastry into a square about 8 inches across. Turn over so that the rolled side is downwards, and using a long knife trim off just enough to give straight edges.

10. Lift the pastry on the rolling-pin and place over a baking-tin so that the points of the pastry overlap the sides of the tin.

11. Arrange the fish mixture in a heap in the centre of the pastry as shown in the diagram.

12. Moisten the edges of the pastry with beaten egg or milk. Lift each corner up over the centre of the fish and press the moistened edges together. This makes a square pastry envelope.

13. Roll the trimmings of pastry out, trim and cut into strips ½ inch wide. Cut across the strips diagonally to make diamond-shaped leaves. Mark the leaves with veins and arrange either over the joins of pastry or between.

14. If the leaves are arranged between the joins flake the joined edges of the pastry envelope with a knife to make a better seal.

15. Brush over the surface of the pie with beaten egg or milk; avoid brushing cut edges of pastry.

16. Bake in a very hot oven for 15 minutes or until the pastry is risen and golden brown. Reduce the heat, cover if necessary with a margarine paper, and allow the pastry to cook through. This will take about 45 minutes in all.

17. Garnish with a sprig of parsley, and serve on a hot meat dish.

18. Parsley or anchovy sauce should be served with Russian Fish Pie. If liked ½ pint of coating sauce may be made by doubling the flour, margarine, and liquid given in the recipe. Take out 2 tablespoonfuls of sauce for moistening the fish, and keep the rest of the sauce to thin down for serving with the pie.

FRYING IN DEEP FAT

Frying in deep fat is an excellent method for thin, quickly cooked foods, but it is both dangerous and extravagant unless proper care is used. If the fat catches fire:

1. Turn off the heat.
2. Cover with a lid, tin-plate, baking-tray, or other flat object.
3. Leave covered until quite cold.

The pan.
1. Use a strong deep pan with a good handle. Light pans become too hot and tip easily.
2. A wire basket to fit inside the pan is used for small coated foods, except those coated in batter which float.

The fat.
1. Use clean dripping or cooking fat. All scraps of fat from meat should be rendered down and strained to add to the deep fat.
2. Strain carefully through a fine strainer or a piece of muslin kept for the purpose after each use.
3. When the fat becomes dirty it can be cleared or clarified. Put the cold fat in the pan and cover with water, bring slowly to the boil, and strain into a deep basin. The fat will set on top, the water will sink to the bottom, and the dirt or sediment will lie on the underside of the fat.
4. Next day, or when the fat is quite set, lift out, scrape away the sediment, and reheat slowly to drive off any remaining water.

5. Fat becomes dirty when it is allowed to become too hot, or when food is badly coated and small bits come away and burn in the fat.

6. Prevent waste of fat by draining the food over the pan for a moment when lifting out.

The frying.

1. Have the fat deep enough to cover the food, but not more than half-way up the pan.

2. Do not have other pans very near when frying.

3. Keep a plate on the rack or as near as possible for putting greasy utensils down.

4. The fat is ready for frying when a slight blue haze rises from it. Hot fat must be watched all the time.

5. Do not splash when putting fried food in the deep fat. Make sure foods are as dry as possible. If the fat bubbles up due to wet food lift the basket a little.

6. Fried foods are always drained before serving on a piece of crumpled kitchen paper on a warm baking-tray.

7. Allow the fat to cool before straining back into the bowl kept specially for the deep fat.

8. Rub the pan out with newspaper before washing.

FISH CROQUETTES

1 lb. white fish—cod, hake, or fresh haddock.

A panada or thick white sauce :

1 oz. margarine.	¼ pt. fish liquor or milk.
1 oz. flour.	1 teasp. chopped parsley.

Salt and pepper.

Flavourings: A few drops of lemon juice, or ½ teasp. anchovy essence.
For coating: Egg and crumbs.

1. *To cook the fish.* Prepare and cook as for Russian Fish Pie, p. 27. An alternative method is to wash and trim the fish, put between two enamel plates, and stand over a pan of boiling water. Allow about 30 minutes. This

method is useful when the oven is not being used for other cooking. The liquor will be fish stock and should be used with equal quantities of milk to make the sauce.

2. Make the thick sauce. Melt the fat, add the flour, and add the fish liquor or milk. Cook thoroughly until the mixture is thick and smooth.

3. Chop the parsley and remove the skin and bones from the fish. Add the parsley and fish to the sauce. Season and taste. The mixture should be firm and evenly mixed.

4. Turn on to a plate and spread flat. Allow to cool.

5. Flour a chopping-board. Scrape the mixture from the plate and make into a fat sausage.

6. Mark and cut into eight even pieces.

7. Shape each piece into a cork-shaped croquette. They should be about 3 inches long with flat ends and smooth round sides.

8. Prepare the coating. (See *Look and Cook*, p. 57, for coating.) Coat each croquette first in the liquid coating and then in the browned crumbs. Press the coating on and re-shape.

9. Prepare the fat for frying, the draining-paper, and a hot dish.

10. When the fat is just smoking-hot put the croquettes in the frying-basket and lower carefully into the fat. Reduce the heat a little and fry until crisp and golden brown. This takes about 3 minutes. Lift the basket out of the fat, tilt slightly, and allow as much fat as possible to drip back into the pan.

11. Lift the croquettes carefully on to the draining-paper. Keep the fried croquettes hot and reheat the fat until it is smoking-hot before frying the rest.

12. Serve the croquettes piled together on a hot dish. Garnish with parsley and serve as soon after frying as possible.

13. Parsley or tomato sauce is served with fish croquettes.

*B

TOMATO SAUCE

½ lb. tomatoes.	A pinch of sugar.
1 small onion.	A blade of mace.
1 small carrot.	A small bay leaf.
1 oz. bacon rinds.	½ pt. stock or water.
1 oz. margarine.	½ oz. flour.
Salt and pepper.	1 tablesp. milk.

To make.

1. Prepare the vegetables. Cut up the onion and carrot, slice the tomatoes.
2. Melt the margarine and add the bacon rinds. Fry the onion and carrot for a few minutes. This gives a good flavour to the sauce. Add the sliced tomatoes, the stock or water, herbs and seasoning. Cover with a lid and leave to simmer until the vegetables are tender, allow 30–40 minutes.
3. Blend the flour with a little cold milk.
4. Strain the vegetables and rub the tender parts through a sieve or strainer. The herbs, bacon rinds, and tomato seeds and skins will be left.
5. Add the blended flour to the sauce, return to the rinsed pan, and stir until it boils. Boil for 3 minutes. Taste, season, and serve.
6. The sauce should be a creamy pouring consistency.

FRIED FISH IN YEAST BATTER

Small thick pieces of fish may be coated in a thick batter and fried in deep fat. A yeast batter makes a delicious coating.
N.B. Read through 'Frying in Deep Fat,' p. 29.

YEAST BATTER

4 oz. flour.	½ oz. yeast.
¼ teasp. salt.	½ teasp. sugar.
¼ pt. milk.	

To make.

1. Cream the yeast with the sugar.
2. Measure the flour and salt and put it to warm.
3. Make the milk just tepid. Pour over the creamed yeast.

4. Make a well in the centre of the flour and add the yeast and milk, mix with a wooden spoon until all the flour has been worked in. Beat slightly, then cover with an enamel plate, and leave in a warm place for 30 minutes.
5. Beat lightly again, add a little more warm milk or water if necessary. The batter should be a thick coating consistency. Leave to stand in a warm place until required.

Note.

Remember the rules for yeast cooking, and avoid great heat and draughts.

TO COAT AND FRY THE FISH

¾ lb. fillet of cod or fresh haddock.   Yeast batter as above.
Lemon and parsley to garnish.   ½ pt. parsley sauce to serve.

To cook.

1. Wash, wipe, and skin the fish. Make quite sure that there are no bones left from filleting.
2. Cut the fish into small thick pieces. Allow about two pieces to each person.
3. Prepare the deep fat for frying, the draining-paper, and a hot dish. No frying-basket is used for foods fried in batter. Have ready a skewer and a fish-slice or draining-spoon—a wire whisk will do if necessary.
4. Make the fat just smoking-hot, coat the fish in the batter, put in two or three pieces at a time. Lift out the fish on the skewer, wrap the batter round it with the wooden spoon, and slide gently into the fat. Fry about half the fish at a time. The coating is best done on top of the stove with the bowl resting on an enamel plate for firmness. Reduce the heat slightly to allow the fish to cook through without over browning.
5. Allow 5–7 minutes for the fish to cook through. Thick pieces take longer than thin ones.
6. Lift out the fish on the draining-spoon, leave to drip a moment, and then place on the draining-paper. Keep the fish hot until it is all ready.

7. Serve on a hot dish, garnish with parsley and quarters of lemon.
8. Serve a flowing parsley or anchovy sauce.

CHEESE EGGS

4 eggs.	1 oz. flour.	¼ teasp. made mustard.
2 oz. cheese.	1 oz. margarine.	Seasoning.
	½ pt. milk.	

To make.

1. Hard-boil 4 eggs. Crack and remove shells, and cut in half lengthways. Arrange cut side down in a deep dish and keep hot.
2. Grate the cheese finely and mix a little mustard with water.
3. Melt the margarine, add the flour to make a roux. Add the milk and cook thoroughly to make a coating-sauce.
4. Add the mustard, cheese, salt, and pepper to the sauce.
5. Pour the cheese sauce over the hard boiled eggs. Garnish with parsley.

Note.

If liked a little cheese may be kept back, mixed with 1 teaspoonful browned breadcrumbs and sprinkled over the surface of the dish. This may then be browned under the grill.

Vegetables for Dinner

CAULIFLOWER

1 large or two medium cauliflowers.
1½ oz. margarine.   1½ oz. flour.   Salt and pepper.
¾ pt. milk and vegetable water mixed.

To cook.

1. Large cauliflowers are usually divided into sprigs for cooking. Small ones may be left whole. Cut off the stalk end, pull apart into sprigs, and wash thoroughly in cold salted water. Keep as much of the tender green part as possible, but throw away any coarse leaves and stalks. Trim off

any badly bruised or discoloured parts of the flower. For boiling whole cauliflowers split the stalk both ways to allow the water to penetrate.

2. Wash at least twice. Autumn cauliflowers may need steeping in salt water for 30 minutes to draw out any insects.

3. Prepare a pan of boiling salted water. Put the cauliflower sprigs in. Put whole cauliflowers head down at first and turn after 10 minutes. Cover with a lid. Bring back to the boil, then lower the heat until the water is just boiling gently. This prevents the flowers from breaking up.

4. Allow 20-30 minutes for cooking. Test the stalk with a skewer or vegetable knife.

5. When the stalk is tender drain the cauliflower very carefully into a colander. Do not break up the flowers. Keep some of the water for making the sauce. Place the colander over the pan and allow to drain for several minutes.

6. Make a smooth coating roux sauce. Season well. Use some of the cauliflower water with the milk.

7. Arrange the cauliflower right side up in a hot vegetable dish. Pour over the sauce so that all the cauliflower is coated. Serve as soon as possible.

Note.

Cauliflower cheese is made in the same way by making a cheese sauce and grilling the top to brown the surface.

LEEKS

Allow 1 large or 2-3 small ones for each person.
Leeks are also coated with white sauce as for cauliflower.

To cook.

1. Cut across the bottom of each leek to about ½ inch up to remove the root.

2. Cut across the top of each leek to remove the leaves so that about 1 inch of green is left.

3. Remove the outside layer and wash very thoroughly under a running tap to remove all grit between the layers.

4. Very large leeks are slit lengthways in half before washing.
5. Prepare a pan with boiling water. Add 1 teaspoonful salt. Use just sufficient water to cover.
6. Put the leeks into the pan. Long ones may need cutting in two. Cover and bring back to the boil, then reduce the heat and allow to simmer.
7. Allow 30–40 minutes, then test with a vegetable knife.
8. When tender drain in a colander. Leave to drain several minutes, standing the colander over the pan and covering the leeks with the lid. Keep some of the water for making the sauce.
9. Place the leeks lengthways in a vegetable dish. Coat evenly with a good white sauce ($\frac{1}{2}$ pint is sufficient), and serve very hot.

CELERY

Celery is cooked in the same way as leeks.

It is usually coated with white sauce and takes about the same time to cook.

Allow two heads or roots of celery for four people.

To prepare.

1. Cut off the root and the green leaves.
2. Pull apart into sticks. Cut up the heart into chunky pieces.
3. Scrub very thoroughly in cold water. Cut off any frosted or discoloured parts. Cut the sticks in two or three.
4. Boil and serve as for leeks.

MARROW

To steam marrow.

1. Wash and peel the marrow. Cut a large one in two or four before peeling.
2. Scoop out the seeds.
3. Cut the marrow up into strips about 2 inches wide by 3 inches long.

4. Prepare a pan of boiling water and choose a steamer with a good lid to fit over the top. Potatoes or other vegetables may be cooked in the water below.
5. Arrange the marrow in the steamer, sprinkle with salt and pepper, and put the steamer carefully over the boiling water.
6. Allow 20–30 minutes. Test with a vegetable knife.
7. When tender remove the steamer and stand it on an enamel plate to drain.
8. Arrange the marrow neatly, rounded side up, in a hot vegetable dish. Coat with sauce and serve as soon as possible.

MARROW IN THE OVEN

Marrow may also be cooked in a moderate oven in a casserole with a lid. Use very little water as the marrow soon shrinks and cooks in its own juice.

Prepare the marrow as for steaming, and use some of the juice from cooking for making the sauce.

BAKED TOMATOES

Allow 1 or 2 tomatoes to each person.
½ oz. margarine. Parsley for garnish.

To cook.

1. Prepare a moderate oven and grease a baking-tin.
2. Choose firm, even-sized tomatoes.
3. Wipe the tomatoes and remove the stalks.
4. Either leave the tomatoes whole or cut across in half.
5. Arrange, cut side up if in half, on the greased tray. Put a tiny knob of margarine on each, or cover with a greased paper.
6. Bake for 10–15 minutes. To test press gently at the base. The tomatoes should be quite whole, but should feel soft when pressed.
7. When cooked lift carefully into a hot vegetable dish and garnish with parsley.

Puddings for Dinner

BAKED APPLES

4 medium-sized cooking apples.
2 tablesp. syrup or 4 level tablesp. sugar.
A little water.

To cook.

1. Prepare a moderate oven.
2. Choose even-sized, well-shaped apples without blemishes.
3. Wash and core the apples. Be careful not to split them. A potato-peeler can be used as a corer.
4. Fit the apples into a fireproof glass dish, or use an enamel pie dish.
5. Pour the syrup over or fill the centres with the sugar. Put 1 or 2 tablespoonfuls water in the bottom of the dish.
6. Bake slowly about 45 minutes.
7. Test with a skewer or vegetable knife. The apples should be tender and beginning to fall.
8. Serve in the same dish if possible to avoid wasting the juice. If necessary use a tablespoon and lift on to a hot serving dish.
9. Serve with custard sauce if liked.

Note.

1. Chopped dates or raisins may also be used to make stuffed apples. Pack the centres before baking, but do not press in too tightly.
2. Some varieties of apple bake much better than others, e.g. Bramley Seedlings and Queens.

APPLE CRACKLE

1 lb. apples.   4 oz. flour.
3 oz. sugar to sweeten.   2 oz. margarine.
     2 oz. sugar.

To make.

1. Prepare a fairly hot oven.
2. Rub the margarine into the flour as for pastry, then add the 2 oz. sugar.

3. Peel and slice the apples. Arrange in a pie dish, sprinkling the 3 oz. sugar in layers between the apples.
4. Pile the rubbed-in mixture on top of the apples. Press lightly into an even shape. Run a fork lengthways across the surface to roughen the mixture.
5. Bake until the apples are tender when tested, and the crackle is golden brown. Allow about 40 minutes.
6. Stand the pie dish on an oval dish and serve with custard sauce.

STEAMED GROUND RICE PUDDING

2 oz. flour.	2 oz. raisins.
2 oz. suet.	$\frac{1}{2}$ teasp. bicarbonate of soda.
2 oz. ground rice or semolina.	2 oz. Demerara sugar.

About $\frac{1}{4}$ pt. milk for mixing.

To make.

1. Fill a steamer and put on to heat. Grease a 1-pint basin and double greaseproof paper to cover.
2. Wash the raisins; dry them in a clean cloth and chop.
3. Sieve the bicarbonate of soda with the flour. Mix in the shredded suet. Add the ground rice.
4. Add the sugar and the raisins and stir in enough milk to obtain a soft dropping consistency. Use a wooden spoon.
5. Turn the mixture into the greased basin. Cover securely with the greased paper by folding in the edge (see *Look and Cook*, p. 40) and steam 2–3 hours. Remember to have a kettle of boiling water ready to fill up the steamer.
6. When the pudding is ready turn off the heat and lift the steamer from the boiling water on to a plate. Remove the lid carefully and lift out the basin.
7. Take off the paper and allow the pudding to shrink a few minutes. Invert a warm serving-dish over the pudding and turn over. Use a clean cloth to lift off the basin.
8. Serve with custard sauce or a sweet white sauce.

QUEEN OF PUDDINGS

3 oz. breadcrumbs.	½ oz. sugar to sweeten.
2 eggs.	1 tablesp. jam.
1 pt. milk.	
½ oz. margarine.	2 oz. castor sugar for the
Rind of 1 lemon or orange.	meringue.

To make.

1. Prepare a moderate oven. Grease a 1½-pint pie dish.
2. Cut off the crusts and rub the bread against a grater to make the breadcrumbs. Put the crumbs in a bowl.
3. Separate the yolks of egg from the whites. Put the whites on to a clean plate ready for whisking.
4. Warm the milk and margarine, pour over the breadcrumbs, add the ½ oz. sugar, the beaten yolks of egg, and grated lemon rind. Leave to soak for 10 minutes.
5. Pour into the greased pie dish and bake until the pudding is set and firm. Allow 30–40 minutes.
6. Spread the jam thinly over the surface of the pudding.
7. Whisk up the whites stiffly. This may be done on a plate with a round-ended knife or in the washed mixing-bowl with a whisk. Continue whisking until the whites are close and stiff.
8. Take out 1 teaspoonful of the sugar and fold the rest lightly into the whites with a tablespoon. Pile the meringue on top of the pudding, cover all the jam. Sprinkle the 1 teaspoonful sugar over the surface.
9. Put the pudding into a moderate oven until the meringue is crisp and a pale golden brown. Allow about 30 minutes.
10. Stand the pie dish on an oval dish to serve.

APPLE FRITTERS

4 oz. yeast batter (see p. 32).	Deep fat for frying.
4 medium apples.	Sugar to coat.

To make.

1. Make the batter as described on p. 32.
2. Core and peel the apples. Cut each apple across into four

    thick rings. Keep the apples in a bowl of cold water until ready for frying.

3. Heat the fat. Do not use a frying-basket for fritters. Prepare a baking-tin with crumpled paper. Put a serving-dish to warm.

4. Dry the apples in a clean cloth and coat two or three rings at a time.

5. Lift the coated rings out of the batter on a skewer, wrap the batter round with a wooden spoon and lower gently into the smoking-hot fat.

6. Fry several rings at once until they are a golden brown. Allow 3–5 minutes. Lift out on a fish-slice or flat whisk, drain a moment, and then keep hot on the crumpled paper until all the rings are fried. Turn out the heat under the fat.

7. Dredge or sprinkle the fritters with sugar and serve on a hot dish as soon as possible.

8. Cool the deep fat before straining.

Note.

    Fritters may also be fried in shallow fat in a frying-pan. Turn over when the first side is cooked.

FRUIT FOOL

| 1 lb. fresh or canned fruit. | $\frac{1}{2}$ pt. custard sauce |
| Sugar to sweeten. | or egg custard. |

To make.

1. Prepare the fruit and stew with a very little water until thick and pulpy.

2. Make $\frac{1}{2}$ pint custard. Stir as it cools to prevent a skin from forming.

3. Sieve the fruit or rub quickly through a stainless strainer. Sweeten to taste. This is now fruit purée, and should measure about $\frac{1}{2}$ pint.

4. When the fruit purée and the custard are both cold, mix together evenly. Add a little colouring if liked. The fruit fool should be smooth and of a thick creamy consistency.

5. Serve in a glass dish or in individual glasses.

6. Serve with sweet biscuits or shortbread fingers.

Note.

1. Most soft fruits are suitable for making into fruit fools, e.g. blackcurrants, raspberries.

2. When using canned or bottled fruits keep back most of the juice and add just sufficient to the sieved fruit to give the correct consistency.

LEMON PIE

4 oz. short crust pastry.	$\frac{1}{2}$ oz. cornflour.
1 lemon.	$\frac{1}{8}$ pt. water ($\frac{1}{2}$ gill).
1 egg.	1 oz. castor sugar for the
3 oz. sugar to sweeten.	meringue.

To make.

1. Prepare a hot oven.

2. Make the pastry. Line a 7-inch sponge-cake tin, a flan ring, or a deep enamel plate. Decorate the edge. Prick the bottom well and bake blind to cook the pastry. (See Flans, p. 61.)

3. Wash the lemon. Grate the rind finely and squeeze out the juice. Separate the egg.

4. Blend the cornflour with the water. This may be done in the saucepan. Add the sugar, lemon rind, and juice.

5. Stir over gentle heat until the mixture boils. Boil for 3 minutes, stirring all the time.

6. Add the beaten yolk of egg. The mixture should be thick and creamy.

7. When the pastry is cooked lift out and reduce the oven to moderate.

8. Pour the mixture into the pastry case, smooth the top.

9. Whip the white of egg stiffly. Whip until it is close and firm. Whisk in the sugar, keeping back 1 teaspoonful.

10. Using a teaspoon place the meringue neatly on top of the lemon filling.

11. Sprinkle the surface with the rest of the sugar.

12. Put back into the oven to become crisp and a very pale golden brown. Allow about 30 minutes.

Afternoon Teas

A selection of recipes for sandwiches, scones, cakes, and biscuits follow; others may be found in *Look and Cook*.

Note.
If it can be afforded butter may be used instead of margarine.

SANDWICH FILLINGS

1. SARDINE AND APPLE

1 small tin of sardines in tomato.
1 small cooked apple.

To make.

1. Lift the sardines on to a plate—remove the tails.
2. Mince the sardines with a fork.
3. Peel and core the apple and cook carefully with 2 table-spoonfuls water and 1 teaspoonful sugar. The cooked apple should be thick in consistency.
4. Mix together the minced sardines with an equal amount of apple.
5. Allow the mixture to cool.

Note.
The apple is used to make the sardines more digestible.

2. CHEESE AND DATE

2 oz. grated cheese.
6 finely chopped dates.
A little cream from the top of the milk.

To make.

1. Grate the cheese.
2. Chop the dates.
3. Mix the two together, adding a little cream or milk to make the mixture spread easily.

3. DATE AND APPLE

1 chopped dessert apple.   8 chopped dates.

To make.

1. Chop the dates.
2. Peel, core, and chop the apple.
3. Mix the two together.

4. MARMITE AND WATERCRESS

1 bunch watercress.   Marmite.

To make.

1. Prepare the watercress carefully (see *Look and Cook*, p. 17). Shred with a knife.
2. Use this between bread and butter spread with Marmite.

5. CUCUMBER AND PARSLEY

Cucumber.   Parsley.   Salt.

To make.

1. Wash the cucumber.
2. Slice thin rounds. Spread these on a dish and sprinkle with salt. Leave to stand $\frac{1}{2}$ hour. Rinse off the salt and drain the cucumber.
3. Pick, wash, dry, and snip the parsley.
4. Use the two together in sandwiches.

SANDWICHES FOR AFTERNOON TEA

A sandwich loaf or rolls are the best kinds of bread to use. The sandwich loaf should be a day old to facilitate neat cutting of the bread, but new rolls are easy to split and butter. Crusts may be removed from the loaf if desired. This should be done after cutting the bread and before buttering to avoid waste of butter and filling. If the whole loaf is to be cut for sandwiches the crusts can conveniently be cut from the loaf before the bread is cut.

To make.

1. Prepare the filling.
2. Soften the butter.
3. Cut and butter the bread—the slices should be about $\frac{1}{8}$ inch thick and evenly sliced.
4. Place a layer of filling on one piece of bread and butter, and press a second piece on top.

5. When all the sandwiches are made pile them evenly together, and with a sharp knife cut them neatly into equal-sized sandwiches. These may be square, triangular, or finger shaped.

6. Stack the sandwiches on a bread plate, and if savoury garnish with a sprig of washed parsley. The sandwiches should be piled rather than spread about the plate as they look more tidy and also are more moist to eat.

Note.

If sandwiches are made long before they are to be served, they should be wrapped in damp greaseproof paper. They are then quite fresh to eat.

BREAD ROLLS

MILK BREAD

½ lb. flour.	½ oz. yeast.
1 oz. fat.	½ teasp. sugar.
½ teasp. salt.	¼ pt. tepid milk.

To make.

1. Put the flour in a warm bowl.
2. Rub in the fat.
3. Make a well in the centre and sprinkle the salt round the edge.
4. Cream the yeast and sugar. Add three-quarters of the tepid liquid and pour this into the well in the flour; cover and stand in a warm place to sponge for 15 minutes.
5. Keep the remaining liquid warm.
6. When the yeast has sponged mix in the remaining liquid gradually, mixing to a light dough. This will be rather sticky at first, but should be beaten well with the hand or a wooden spoon, and gradually it becomes smooth and can then be kneaded.
7. When quite smooth cover and leave to rise in a warm place. After covering, the bowl may be wrapped in a clean cloth or a double sheet of newspaper to exclude draught, which would spoil the finished bread.

8. When the dough has doubled in size—this takes about 1 hour—lift on to a lightly floured board and knead lightly.
9. Divide into 12 or 16 pieces.
10. Knead each piece into a round on the floured board, and then roll with the palm of the hand on the board into 3-inch fingers.
11. Place on a warm, greased baking-tray. They should almost touch each other so that they keep a good shape, rise into each other, and in consequence have soft edges when split apart after baking.
12. Cover with a clean cloth, and prove in a warm place 15–20 minutes. Brush with milk after proving.
13. Bake towards the top of a hot oven 10–15 minutes until gold and firm underneath.
14. After baking remove at once to a cooling-tray, and rub over with a margarine paper to make them soft on top.

Note.

If yeast rolls are to be made in a short space of time the rising in the bowl may be omitted, i.e. 7 and 8 above. After kneading shape the rolls, following the instructions 9 to 14. These rolls will be good to eat, though not quite so light nor evenly risen as when the full time can be given.

BAKING-POWDER ROLLS

These are quickly made and make a change.

½ lb. flour.	½ teasp. salt.
2 teasp. baking-powder.	1 oz. fat.
About ¼ pt. cold milk.	

To make.

1. Prepare a hot oven, and grease a baking-tray.
2. Sieve together the flour, baking-powder, and salt.
3. Rub in the fat.
4. Sprinkle in the milk and mix to a light dough. This should be slightly sticky.
5. Lift on to a lightly floured board. Toss over to coat with flour.
6. Divide into 12 pieces.
7. Shape each piece into a round in a lightly floured hand. Then roll with the palm of the hand on a board into 3-inch fingers.

8. Place close together on the greased tin.   Brush with milk.
9. Bake at once towards the top of a hot oven for 10–15 minutes.
10. When firm and gold lift on to a cooling-tray and rub over
    with a margarine paper.

Note.
   These rolls should be eaten fresh.

AFTERNOON TEA SCONES
(makes 12)

½ lb. flour.
1½ oz. margarine.
1 oz. sugar.
½ teasp. salt.
1 teasp. cream of tartar ⎫ or 1 heaped teasp. baking-powder.
½ teasp. bicarbonate of soda ⎭
1 oz. fruit.
1 egg (may be omitted).
Milk to mix: ¾ gill if an egg is used.
                1 gill if no egg is used.

To make.

1. Prepare a hot oven and grease a baking-tray.
2. Sieve into the baking-bowl the flour, salt, cream of tartar,
   and bicarbonate of soda.
3. Clean the fruit.
4. Rub the fat into the flour, etc.
5. Add the fruit and sugar.
6. Beat up the egg and scatter it over, together with enough
   milk to mix to a soft dough, mixing quickly with a knife.
7. Lift on to a lightly floured board.   Shape quickly into a
   neat shape.
8. Press with the hand or roll out, keeping the dough 1 inch
   in thickness.
9. Lightly flour a 1¼-inch cutter and stamp out rounds,
   placing them on the greased tin.   Repeat until all the
   dough is used.
10. Bake at once near the top of the oven, about 10 minutes,
    until firm in the centre bottom and a golden brown.
11. Lift at once on to a cooling-tray.

WHOLEMEAL SCONES

¼ lb. plain flour.	½ teasp. salt.
¼ lb. wholemeal flour.	1 teasp. cream of tartar.
1½ oz. margarine.	½ teasp. bicarbonate of soda.
1 oz. sugar.	1 gill milk.

Make and bake exactly as for Afternoon Tea Scones.

SYRUP OR TREACLE SCONES

¼ lb. plain flour.	½ teasp. ginger.
¼ lb. wholemeal flour.	½ teasp. cream of tartar.
1½ oz. margarine.	½ teasp. bicarbonate of soda.
1 oz. sugar.	1 tablesp. treacle.

Short ¼ pt. milk.

Make and bake exactly as for Afternoon Tea Scones. The treacle should be melted and added before the milk.

DROPPED SCONES or SCOTCH PANCAKES
(makes 16)

½ lb. flour.	½ teasp. bicarbonate of soda.
Pinch of salt.	2 oz. sugar.
1 teasp. cream of tartar.	1 egg.

About ¼ pt. milk.

To make.

1. Have ready a clean electric hot-plate, strong frying-pan or girdle, and a piece of lard and lard paper for greasing.
2. Sieve together the flour, salt, cream of tartar, and crushed bicarbonate of soda.
3. Add the sugar. Mix together.
4. Make a well in the centre and add the well-beaten egg and most of the milk.
5. Mix in the flour, etc., and add more milk to mix to a thick pouring consistency. Beat thoroughly.
6. Make the hot-plate, frying-pan, or girdle hot, grease over.
7. When faintly smoking, drop on the mixture from a dessert-spoon. On a girdle four may be cooked at once, but fewer on a hot-plate or frying-pan.

8. Regulate the heat so that the scones rise and bubbles appear all over the top by the time the part touching the hot-plate is a golden brown colour.

9. With a palette knife turn over and cook the other side until a good colour and the sides of the scone are firm to touch.

10. Lift on to a tea-towel on a cooling-tray.

11. Grease the hot-plate each time.

12. If necessary trim the edges of the scones with scissors after frying, and after switching off rub down the hot-plate with a crumpled paper and later wipe over when cool.

Note.

Left-over dropped scones may be toasted the following day.

SALLY LUNN

½ lb. flour.	½ oz. yeast.
½ teasp. salt.	½ teasp. sugar.
1½ oz. margarine.	1 egg.
Short ¼ pt. tepid milk.	

To make.

1. Warm and grease a suitable cake-tin about the size of a 1-pint basin, or a ½-lb. loaf-tin.

2. Sieve the flour and salt and rub in the margarine.

3. Cream the yeast and sugar, add the beaten egg, and half the measured tepid milk.

4. Cover and leave to sponge 10–15 minutes.

5. Mix to a soft consistency, adding more warm milk if required.

6. Beat well. Knead lightly into a round.

7. Place in the tin.

8. Cover with a tea-towel, leave to rise in a warm place until it is double the size.

9. Bake in a fairly hot oven for 30–40 minutes, till golden brown and hollow when tested by tapping gently underneath.

Note.

Sally Lunn should be sliced and buttered on the day on which it is made. It is served as a change from scones.

CAKES AND BUNS

CHELSEA BUNS
(makes 12)

½ lb. flour.	*Filling*	*Glaze*
½ teasp. salt.	½ oz. melted margarine.	2 teasp. sugar.
½ oz. yeast.	1 oz. sugar.	1 tablesp. water.
1 teasp. sugar.	2 oz. currants and sultanas.	
1 egg.		
¾ gill warm milk.		
1 oz. sugar.		
1 oz. margarine.		

To make.

1. Sieve the flour and salt into a warm bowl.
2. Rub in the margarine, add the 1 oz. of sugar and mix.
3. Make a well in the centre.
4. Cream the yeast and 1 teaspoonful sugar. Pour into the well together with the beaten egg and ⅛ pint tepid milk.
5. Cover and leave to sponge 10–15 minutes.
6. Mix up to a soft dough, adding more of the warm milk if necessary—the dough must not be stiff. Beat until smooth.
7. Cover, wrap up to exclude draughts, and put in a warm place to rise until twice the size.
8. Melt the margarine in a small pan, and prepare the fruit and extra sugar for the filling.
9. Grease a suitable tin to hold twelve buns. A baking-tray can be used, but the following keep the buns a better shape—a tin 10 inches by 7 inches, approximately, and 2 inches deep would take the twelve buns, four down the long side and three the other way, or a 7-inch round cake-tin makes an attractive ring of seven buns round the edge and one in the centre; the other four could then be baked together in a smaller tin. After greasing, the tin must be warmed.
10. Lift the dough on to a floured board. Handle carefully, as it is inclined to be sticky.

11. Knead lightly, then roll into an oblong about 12 inches by 9 inches, having the long side towards the worker.

12. Brush with the melted margarine.

13. Sprinkle with the fruit and then with the sugar.

14. Damp the furthest edge, then roll the dough from the near edge to the damped edge, pressing carefully together to seal at the far side.

15. Cut the roll in two equal pieces, then each piece into six buns.

16. Lift each bun in turn, and if there is a little margarine left in the pan, brush round the edge of the buns and place them in the tin with the edges nearly touching. This makes them easy to break apart neatly when baked.

17. Cover and leave to prove 15–20 minutes.

18. Bake in a fairly hot oven for about $\frac{1}{2}$ hour. Melt the sugar and water together for the glaze and brush over the buns 5 minutes before they are ready. They should be an even golden colour and firm at the edges and where they join.

19. Remove carefully to a cooling-tray.

20. Split apart when cold.

FEATHER-ICED COFFEE-CREAM SANDWICH CAKE

Victoria Sandwich	*Plainer Recipe*
2 eggs.	2 eggs.
4 oz. margarine.	4 oz. margarine.
4 oz. castor sugar.	4 oz. castor sugar.
4 oz. flour.	6 oz. self-raising flour.
1 small teasp. baking-powder.	Milk to mix.
Milk if required.	

Cream Filling	*Glacé Icing*
1 oz. margarine.	4 heaped tablesp. sieved icing sugar.
1$\frac{1}{2}$ oz. sieved icing sugar.	Hot water added from a teasp. to mix.
1 small teasp. Nescafe powder.	

FEATHER-ICED COFFEE-CREAM SANDWICH.

To make.

1. Prepare a fairly hot oven.
2. Grease two sandwich tins 7 inches in diameter.
3. Thoroughly cream the margarine and sugar until light and creamy.
4. Gradually beat in the well-beaten eggs a little at a time.
5. Stop beating and carefully stir in the sieved flour and baking-powder, and enough milk to mix to a soft dropping consistency.
6. Divide the mixture equally between the two tins and spread level.
7. Bake in the oven between the centre and top for 20–25 minutes. After 10 minutes reduce the heat to moderate, and if the tins are not on the same shelf change over, taking care not to shake the tins.
8. When firm in the centre and evenly golden brown, take from the oven and turn out carefully on to a wire tray.
9. Allow to cool.

To make the cream.

1. Cream the margarine and icing sugar until light and creamy.

2. Mix in the Nescafé powder.
3. Add 1 teaspoonful cream from the top of the milk if available.

To make the glacé icing.

1. Sieve the icing sugar into a 1-pint basin.
2. Add hot water from a pan, a very little at a time, using a teaspoon.
3. Mix with a wooden spoon until the icing coats the spoon thickly—the ridges should disappear when the icing is dropped back from the spoon to the basin.
4. Take 2 teaspoonfuls of this icing into a cup, and add ½ teaspoonful Nescafé powder to this to mix to a rich brown colour.

To complete the cake.

1. Make a paper piping bag (see p. 130), cut off ½ inch at the bottom and insert a No. 2 plain writing tube. If this is not available the paper piping bag alone may be used, but in this case cut off only ⅛ inch at the bottom, to allow a thick line of icing to be squeezed from the end.
2. Scrape the coffee icing from the cup into this bag, and fold down the top ready for piping. Have a skewer ready to use with this later.
3. Place one sandwich cake upside-down on a suitable plate. Spread on the coffee-cream. Place the second cake right side up on the top of the cream.
4. Beat the white glacé icing again and spread it quickly over the cake, keeping the icing just to the edge.
5. Quickly, with the coffee icing in the bag, pipe a straight line down the centre of the cake. Then still working quickly, pipe lines an equal distance apart to the right-hand edge of the cake. Then quickly turn the cake and do the same again until there are parallel coffee-coloured lines down the cake (see diagram overleaf).

6. Quickly turn the cake so that the lines are across in front of you, and, with the skewer, lightly draw a line down the centre of the icing.

7. Turn the cake round again and draw lines on either side of the first, making these the same distance apart as the piped lines.

8. Turn the cake again, and repeat towards the sides. Continue to turn the cake and repeat until the edges are reached (see photograph, p. 52).

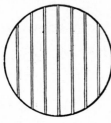 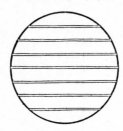 

Pipe lines down the cake.	Turn the lines sideways.	Quickly draw a fine skewer lightly down the centre. Repeat according to the instructions until the cake looks like the photograph on p. 52.

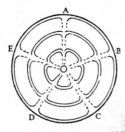

ALTERNATIVE DESIGNS

1. *Flower*. Pipe three circles and a small dot in the centre. Draw the skewer lightly from A, B, C, D, and E, to centre dot.

2. *Catherine Wheel*. Pipe a spiral, starting in the centre. Draw the skewer either from the outside in, or the reverse, for pretty effects.

To FEATHER-ICE

ALTERNATIVE FILLINGS AND DECORATIONS

1. *Feather-iced vanilla-cream cake.*

    Instead of the coffee put 4 drops vanilla essence in the cream, and in the piping icing use a few drops of cochineal colouring to make a deep pink icing for piping instead of the brown.

2. *Feather-iced chocolate-cream cake.*

    Make the cream and beat in 2 teaspoonfuls cocoa, and colour the piping icing brown with a few drops of brown colouring.

Note.

Instead of feather icing, the following are attractive ways of varying the cake:

1. *Decorated coffee-cream cake.*

    Sandwich the cakes with coffee-cream (see pp. 51 and 52). Add sufficient Nescafé powder from a teaspoon to all the glacé icing (see pp. 51 and 53) to make it an attractive coffee colour. Beat the icing well to mix in the coffee evenly and have it a coating consistency, then spread it over the cake to the edge. Place half-walnuts evenly round the edge.

2. *Decorated vanilla-cream cake.*

    Sandwich the cake with vanilla-cream (see above). Mix up the glacé icing (see pp. 51 and 53), keeping all of it white. Beat well and have it a coating consistency, then spread it over the cake to the edge. Place glacé cherries evenly round the edge.

3. *Decorated chocolate-cream cake.*

    Sandwich the cakes with chocolate-cream (see above).

Chocolate Icing

1¼ tablesp. water.	2 oz. icing sugar.
1 oz. plain chocolate.	3 drops vanilla essence.

c

To make.

1. Break up the chocolate and put it in a small pan with the water.
2. Place over a very gentle heat and melt and bring just to the boil (avoid over-heating as this makes the chocolate icing dull and not glossy). Remove from the heat.
3. Add the sieved icing sugar gradually, beating it well in and using enough to make a coating consistency. Beat well to produce a gloss.
4. Spread over the cake.
5. Decorate with silver balls or 'Smarties.'

Note.

1. When a cake is to be glacé-iced, a collar of double greaseproof paper may be pinned tightly round the cake sides, allowing $\frac{1}{4}$ inch to stand above the top edge of the cake. This prevents the icing running down the sides of the cake. It should be left in position until the icing is set and then should be carefully peeled away and the pin should be put safely away. A collar is not possible if the cake is feather-iced, as the paper gets in the way of the feathering. This is a specially useful hint if the cake to be iced is not quite flat.
2. Small buns in paper cases may be made instead of sandwich cakes, using the Victoria Sandwich recipe (see p. 51). The cases should stand on a baking-tray and should be filled three-quarters full of mixture. These should be baked in a fairly hot oven for 15–20 minutes. They may then be iced with any of the glacé icings, or they could be made into butterfly cakes.

BUTTERFLY CAKES

1. Make a flavoured butter-cream (see pp. 51 and 52).
2. When the buns are cold, using a vegetable knife, cut rounds out of the centres of the tops of the buns.
3. Fill the hollows with cream.
4. Carefully cut the little cake-rounds in two and put back into the cream with the cut edges touching.
5. Dredge the tops with icing sugar.

Note.

When dredging anything small with sugar, always stand the things over paper, then spare sugar may be put back into the jar.

ORANGE CAKE

4 oz. margarine.
4 oz. castor sugar.
6 oz. flour   } or 6 oz. self-
1 teasp. baking-powder } raising flour.
Grated rind of 1 orange.
2 eggs.
1 tablesp. orange juice.
Milk to mix.

ORANGE GLACÉ ICING

4 tablesp. sieved icing sugar.
Strained orange juice to mix to coating consistency.

Decorations
Flowers made from peel.

To make.

1. Wash the orange, and with a potato-peeler cut two strips of rind to use in decorating the cake.
2. Grate the rest of the rind.
3. Line a 6-inch cake-tin with greased greaseproof paper (see *Look and Cook*, p. 118).
4. Make as for rich cake mixture (see *Look and Cook*, p. 124). Stir in the orange rind and juice with the sieved flour and baking-powder.
5. Mix to a soft dropping consistency with milk. Place in the tin.
6. Bake just above the centre of a moderately hot oven for $\frac{3}{4}$–1 hour.
7. When cold, strip off the greaseproof paper. Pin round a double band of greaseproof.
8. Spread over the orange glacé icing. Allow to set.
9. Decorate with orange-peel flowers: cut strips, then diamonds, then make flowers.

CHOCOLATE CAKE

4 oz. margarine.
4 oz. castor sugar.
2 eggs.
4 oz. flour.

1 oz. cocoa.
$\frac{1}{2}$ teasp. baking-powder.
3 drops vanilla essence.
Milk to mix.

Make as Victoria Sandwich (see p. 51). When cold sandwich together with chocolate-cream (see p. 55) and ice with chocolate glacé icing (see p. 55).

CHERRY CAKE

4 oz. margarine.
4 oz. castor sugar.
2 eggs.

8 oz. self-raising flour or $\begin{cases} 6 \text{ oz. flour.} \\ 2 \text{ oz. ground rice.} \\ 1 \text{ teasp. baking-powder.} \end{cases}$

Pinch of salt.
3 oz. glacé cherries.
4 drops vanilla essence.
Milk to mix.

To make.

1. Prepare a moderate oven.
2. Line a 2-lb. loaf-tin with greased greaseproof paper.
3. Make as for rich cake mixture (see *Look and Cook*, p. 124).
4. Dredge the top of the mixture lightly with castor sugar.
5. Bake for about 1 hour until firm to the touch and golden brown.

COCO-NUT PYRAMIDS
(makes 8)

4 oz. desiccated coco-nut.   2 oz. sugar.
1 beaten egg.

To make.

1. Prepare a moderate oven. Grease a baking-tray.
2. Mix the coco-nut and sugar.
3. Beat the egg well and add it to the coco-nut and sugar, mixing well with a fork.
4. Dip an egg-cup in cold water to damp it; fill with the mixture, pressing down gently.
5. Invert loosely in the cupped palm of the hand, shake and lift on to the tin.
6. Repeat 4 and 5. Bake carefully about 20 minutes.

BRANDY SNAP

3 oz. margarine.   2 oz. sugar.
3 oz. syrup.   2 oz. flour.
½ teasp. ginger if liked.

Note. To make successfully:
1. Weigh accurately.
2. Read the instructions through before you begin.

To make.

1. Prepare a fairly hot oven.
2. Grease two baking-trays.
3. Lightly flour the scale-pan and weigh the syrup accurately, and put it into a saucepan with the weighed margarine and sugar.
4. Weigh the flour and sieve on to a paper from which it may be sifted into the pan after the syrup, margarine, and sugar have been melted.
5. Melt together the syrup, margarine, and sugar over a very gentle heat, taking care not to boil. Remove from the heat.
6. Sift in the flour and mix with a wooden spoon.
7. Put the mixture in teaspoonfuls on to the prepared tins, spacing them 2 inches apart, putting the first tin in the oven as soon as it is filled; then fill the second tin whilst these are baking.
8. Bake carefully near the top of a fairly hot oven for 3-4 minutes, until they are toffee brown. Meantime have ready a wooden spoon and a knife.
9. Lift the first tin from the oven when ready, not forgetting the other tin shortly after. Allow the brandy snaps to cool slightly, then loosen quickly and carefully with a knife.
10. Quickly lift one piece and roll it round the wooden spoon handle, having the upper side from the tin outside on the roll. Slip off and quickly roll all the others.
11. Repeat with the second tin.
12. If liked, mock cream may be piped in the ends.

MOCK CREAM

2 oz. margarine } creamed together.
2 oz. icing sugar }

½ oz. cornflour } blended and carefully cooked as a blancmange.
¼ pt. milk }

3–4 drops vanilla essence.

To make.

1. Allow the cornflour mixture to cool. Remove the skin.
2. Whisk this mixture a little at a time into the creamed margarine and sugar. Do not add too much at once or the mixture will curdle.
3. Flavour with 3 or 4 drops vanilla essence.

High Teas and Suppers

TARTS, FLANS, AND SAVOURY DISHES

MOCK BAKEWELL TART

4 oz. short pastry.   Apricot jam.

Filling.

2 oz. margarine.   1 oz. ground rice or semolina.
2 oz. sugar.   ¼ teasp. baking powder.
1 egg.   2 drops almond essence.
2 oz. flour.   A little milk if required.

To make.

1. Prepare a fairly hot oven.
2. Make the pastry.
3. Make the filling as for rich cake mixture.
4. Stand a flan-ring or 7-inch sandwich-tin on a baking-tray and line this with the pastry.

To line a flan-ring (or sandwich-tin) with pastry.

1. Shape the pastry into a neat round on a lightly floured board.

2. Roll out, keeping a neat round shape and avoiding cracks in the pastry, until the pastry is the size of the base of the flan-ring plus the sides and $\frac{1}{4}$ inch extra.

3. Carefully lift the pastry on the rolling-pin and lower it into the flan-ring.

4. Ease the pastry carefully so that it is evenly placed and fitting well into the angle of the ring and baking-tray.

5. Slightly bend the top edge of the pastry over the top edge of the flan-ring.

6. Place the rolling-pin firmly across the centre of the ring, and roll off the projecting pastry away from the worker.

7. Turn the baking-tray and repeat this process with the other half. Use the trimmings for biscuits or tarts.

To finish the Mock Bakewell Tart.

1. Spread the bottom of the pastry with apricot jam.

2. Cover the top of the jam with all the cake mixture, spreading evenly in the pastry case.

3. Bake above the centre of the oven for about 30 minutes until the pastry is cooked and the cake mixture firm to the touch in the centre. Reduce the heat after 20 minutes, to cook without over-browning.

4. Lift off the flan-ring and remove the tart with a fish-slice to a suitable plate. Serve hot or cold.

Note.

1. If a sandwich-tin has been used, turn out carefully, as for cake, reversing the tart on to a cooling-tray. Then serve.

2. Other tarts, see index, and also *Look and Cook.*

FRUIT FLAN

FLAN PASTRY

4 oz. flour.	1 teasp. sugar.
Pinch of salt.	1 egg yolk.
2 oz. margarine.	Very little cold water.

FRUIT FLAN

To make.

1. Prepare a fairly hot oven.　Grease a baking-tray and place the flan-ring on it.
2. Sieve the flour and salt.
3. Rub in the fat.
4. Add the sugar and mix with a knife.
5. Add the beaten egg-yolk and enough water added from a teaspoon to mix to a stiff paste.
6. Knead lightly until smooth.
7. Fit the flan-ring (see p. 60).
8. Prick the base of the pastry.
9. Grease a round of greaseproof paper the size of the flan-ring base plus 2 inches extra all round.
10. Crumple this paper and place with the greased side down to the pastry inside the ring.
11. Fill with rice or butter-beans or crusts of bread (kept in a jar for the purpose) to keep the bottom flat.　This is known as baking 'blind.'
12. Bake above the centre of a fairly hot oven until the pastry is firm—about 15 minutes.
13. Carefully lift out the paper with the beans.

14. Return the flan to the oven and bake carefully until the pastry in the bottom is cooked.
15. Lift off the flan-ring, and with a knife and fish-slice lift the flan case to a cooling-tray. The flan may be filled when cold or placed in a tin and used as required in a day or two.

FRUIT FOR THE FLAN

1. A small can of fruit may be used, draining off the syrup and making a glaze (see below) with this.
2. Carefully stewed fruit may be used if the fruit is kept whole —$\frac{1}{2}$ lb. fruit is usually sufficient. Stones should be removed from cherries with a cherry stoner, from plums by carefully cutting and removing the stones. The juice is used for the glaze (see below).
3. Fresh uncooked fruit may be used—oranges sliced in rings, raspberries and strawberries washed and used whole. In this case the glaze is made from $\frac{1}{4}$ pint of water, in which the rind only of the orange is simmered to extract the flavour, or a dozen extra raspberries or six strawberries simmered similarly to extract the flavour and then strained to produce the necessary liquid for the glaze.

To fill and glaze the flan.
1. Place the flan case on a suitable plate.
2. Arrange the fruit in a neat design to fill the case. Sprinkle uncooked fruit lightly with castor sugar.
3. Blend 1 teaspoonful of cornflour or arrowroot in a small saucepan with a little of the $\frac{1}{4}$ pint of juice needed for the glaze.
4. When smooth add the rest of the juice.
5. Stir over gentle heat until boiling, and cook for a few minutes. If made with arrowroot the glaze will be sparkling clear, but with cornflour not quite so bright.
6. Taste, adding more sugar if necessary and definitely adding

*c

sugar to sweeten the glaze made for the uncooked fruit. A drop or two of suitable colouring may be added if necessary.

7. Boil the glaze to a coating consistency—if too stiff thin with a little juice or water.
8. Coat over the whole surface of the fruit in the flan.
9. Serve when cold.

Savoury High Tea or Supper Dishes

BAKED HAM WITH APPLE SAUCE

1 lb. ham cut as one $\frac{1}{2}$-in. slice or rasher.

To cook.

1. Remove the rind of the ham with scissors.
2. Just cover the bottom of a suitably sized roasting-tin with a film of water. Place the ham in this.
3. Cover with an inverted tin, plate, or lid.
4. Place in the centre of a moderate oven.
5. Cook for about $\frac{3}{4}$ hour, then remove the lid and allow the upper side to brown very slightly.
6. Serve on a hot meat dish with the gravy from the tin poured over the ham.

APPLE SAUCE

1 lb. cooking apples.   4 tablesp. water.
1 oz. sugar.

To make.

1. Peel, core, and slice the apples.
2. Place with the water in a suitable pan.
3. Cover and stew gently until well pulped.
4. Beat carefully with a wooden spoon. Add up to 1 oz. sugar if the apples are sour.
5. Serve.

LIVER AND BACON PIE

1 lb. calf's liver.	1 heaped tablesp. flour.
6 oz. fat bacon.	Seasoning.

Water or stock.

To make.

1. Trim, wash, and slice the liver.
2. Remove bacon rind and slice the bacon.
3. Mix flour, pepper, and salt on a plate.
4. Coat the liver with the seasoned flour.
5. Put the liver and bacon in layers in the pie dish, finishing with a layer of bacon.
6. Blend any flour left on the plate with a little of the stock or water, pour this into the pie and fill up with more to the top of the liver.
7. Cover the pie dish with a lid or a double greased greaseproof paper.
8. Cook in a very moderate oven for $2\frac{1}{2}$–3 hours.
9. Serve hot or cold, preferably cold.

POTATO FLAN

POTATO FLAN CASE

$1\frac{1}{2}$ lb. potatoes.	2 teasp. beaten egg.
$\frac{1}{2}$ oz. margarine.	1 tablesp. milk.

Filling: 1 lb. mixed cooked diced vegetables.
(e.g. 1 carrot, 1 small turnip, a few peas, kidney beans, etc., or 1 tin mixed vegetables.)

Sauce: 1 oz. flour.
$\frac{1}{2}$ pt. milk.
$\frac{1}{2}$ teasp. mixed mustard. . Seasoning.
2 oz. cheese.
The remainder of the beaten egg.

To make.

1. Peel the potatoes. Cook in salted water. Drain well and dry. Then add the margarine, beaten egg, and milk, and mash well together.

2. Grease a loose-bottomed cake-tin about 7 inches by 3 inches and coat round inside with browned bread-crumbs, tapping off any surplus crumbs.

3. Pack a layer of the potato mixture on the bottom and up the sides of the tin.

4. Mark round the top edge with a fork.

5. Bake in a fairly hot oven about $\frac{1}{2}$ hour, until set and golden brown on top.   Reduce the oven heat to moderate.

6. Invert a 1-pint basin.   Carefully stand the loose-bottomed tin on this, lowering the tin side steadily down to the table.

7. With a fish-slice lift the flan from the tin bottom straight to a large hot fireproof plate placed closely beside it.

8. Arrange the vegetables attractively in the flan.

9. Make a blended sauce with the flour and milk, and when cooked add the mixed mustard, a little seasoning, most of the grated cheese, and remains of the beaten egg.   Mix well until smooth.

10. Coat over the vegetables with the sauce, sprinkle a little cheese over.   Return the dish to the oven to heat through and brown the top.

11. Thin any remaining sauce and reheat and serve in a sauce-boat.

12. Garnish the flan with parsley and serve.

CHEESE PASTRY FLAN

4 oz. flour.
Pinch of salt.
2 oz. margarine.
2 oz. grated cheese.
Very little water to mix.

To make.

1. Sieve together the flour and salt.
2. Rub in the fat.
3. Add the finely grated cheese.
4. Add 3–4 teaspoonfuls cold water to mix to a very stiff dough.

5. Roll out, line the flan-ring, and bake 'blind,' i.e. without filling in it (see instruction for fruit flan case, p. 62).
6. Fill with cooked vegetables, and coat with sauce as in the previous recipe for potato flan.

Note.

1. The savoury fillings for these two flans may be varied by using such things as cooked mushrooms and chopped cooked ham.
2. The cheese pastry recipe may also be used for cheese straws, cheese biscuits, and other simple cheese savouries.

FISH, OR FISH AND CHEESE PUDDING

6–8 oz. cooked fish, or 4–6 oz. cooked fish and 2 oz. grated cheese.
1 oz. flour.
1 oz. margarine.
½ pt. milk.
Seasoning.
1 egg (may be omitted for economy).

To make.

1. Remove the skin and bones from the cooked fish and grate the cheese if used.
2. Make a well-seasoned roux sauce.
3. Stir in the fish.
4. Separate the yolk from the white of the egg and beat and mix in the yolk.
5. Just before cooking, whisk the egg-white stiffly and fold it into the mixture.
6. Pour into a greased pie dish and put sliced tomatoes in a line down the centre.
7. Bake in a hot oven for 20–25 minutes, until set and golden brown.
8. Serve at once garnished with parsley.

Note.

1. This dish may be prepared during the morning's cooking as far as item 5. The last four instructions can then be quickly carried out in the evening.
2. Four tomatoes may be washed and baked whole to serve with the fish

pudding. Stand them on a film of water on an enamel plate and bake in the same oven.

3. For substantial helpings for four people, double the stated quantities, using 1 or 2 eggs according to what can be spared.

4. If left-over fish is used, then all milk must be used in the sauce, but if a piece of fish is baked specially for this, then use the liquor plus milk to make up the necessary measurement for the sauce.

5. The cheese makes rather tasteless fish more interesting.

SAVOURY OMELET

(A savoury supper for two people)

3 eggs.	¼ teasp. salt.
1 oz. margarine or butter.	pepper.
2 teasp. chopped parsley } if liked.	
Pinch of herbs	

To make.

1. Beat the eggs sufficiently to bind the yolk and white, add the seasoning, parsley, herbs, and half the margarine cut in small pieces.

2. Melt the other half of the margarine in a large frying-pan or omelet-pan. Tilt to grease round the base and sides of the pan. When hot pour in the mixture.

3. With a tablespoon, draw cuts through the mixture until almost setting; this allows the liquid part to run through and cook.

4. Leave undisturbed until set.

5. Loosen the edges with a palette knife and shake the bottom carefully to loosen.

6. Fold over in two, or fold in three.

7. Slip on to a hot meat dish. Garnish with parsley and serve at once.

Note.

1. A previously prepared filling may be placed on the omelet before folding, e.g. chopped cooked ham or chopped cooked mushrooms.

2. Sliced tomatoes may be placed over the top of the omelet when it is almost set. They should be seasoned and then put under the grill for a few minutes to cook. The omelet should then be loosened, folded, garnished, and served.

2

PLANNING SPECIAL MEALS

Packed Meals

PACKED meals must be taken by the worker who has no facility for obtaining a midday meal in a canteen or suitable restaurant, and who because of time or distance cannot get home. A packed meal is often taken when travelling, and sometimes it is just packed for the fun of having a meal out of doors and takes the form of a picnic lunch or tea.

GENERAL RULES TO FOLLOW

1. Plan a balanced meal.
2. Include a hot drink if it will be difficult to obtain one.
3. Prepare things which pack conveniently, remembering things which can be made in small dishes or on saucers.
4. Pack suitably for the occasion, remembering things available for the purpose: waxed bags saved from breakfast cereal packets, cellophane bags, plastic bags (which may be sponged and dried and used over and over again), tin boxes, rucksacks, bicycle baskets, picnic hampers; thermos flasks for drinks, and broad-necked ones which will either keep soup or fried bacon and sausage and tomato hot, or ice-cream in an unmelted condition for several hours.

A. SUGGESTIONS FOR PACKED MEALS FOR THE WORKER

Avoid over-starchy meals, thinking carefully of balance. It may be possible to give small dishes or basins of food to be reheated, but if this is impossible a cooked dinner must be given in the evening. If sandwiches are given margarine and butter may be mixed to make the butter go further, or good beef or pork dripping, with or without Marmite, makes a tasty substitute.

71

SAVOURY THINGS TO PACK

1. Meat and vegetable pies—any sort of cooked meat with gravy, layered with cooked vegetables, and covered with mashed potatoes.
2. Sausage, baked beans, and potato pie—layers of sliced fried sausages with baked beans covered with mashed potatoes.
3. Cheese and onion and potato pie—layers of shredded cheese, onion, and potato in a greased dish, finishing with grated cheese mixed with a teaspoonful of raspings on the top. The pie should be baked until the potato is soft, and when reheated 2 tablespoonfuls of milk should be added.
4. Cornish pasties (see *Look and Cook*).
5. Sausage rolls (see *Look and Cook*).
6. Fish pie (see *Look and Cook*).

SAVOURY SANDWICHES

For fillings see Sandwich Fillings, p. 43. Remember too the use of chutney with sliced meat, mustard with cooked ham, and a little mint sauce with sliced mutton.

SWEET THINGS TO PACK

1. Fruit tarts on saucers. 3 oz. pastry will make a top and bottom crust, and any type of fruit with sugar may be used inside. Do not put water in the tart. The juice will then be a thick syrup and the tart can be conveniently carried on its saucer in greaseproof paper. Treacle, jam, and curd tarts may also be made on saucers.
2. Jam, sweetened apple or date or dried fruit turnover. Eccles cakes or Banbury puffs.
3. Biscuits, plain cake, e.g. rock cakes or date cake, gingerbread or parkin.

Note.

The housewife would always make an extra portion of anything she was making for the family dinner at home, so that the worker could either have it reheated in the evening or take it the following day for dinner. If making a pie for the family, extra pastry could be made and used for a saucer-pie for the worker.

B. Suggestions for Packed Meals for a Journey

Small neat packages are usually the most appreciated, consisting of things which are easy to unpack and convenient to eat. Sometimes buttered bread, spread with Marmite, to be eaten with cheese sections or a tomato are a change from sandwiches.

Avoid iced cakes and those filled with soft cream, also avoid very crumbly pastries; otherwise there are many biscuits and cakes from which to select. If a flask is packed, an unbreakable beaker is useful, as this can be filled less than half full if a drink is taken in a moving train. A small lid or an overfull cup easily spills. A paper serviette should be packed with the traveller's meal.

C. Suggestions for Packed Meals for Picnics

Consider the type of picnic, whether on foot, bicycle, or in a car, and select food and ways of packing which are suitable. If the meal is to be packed for more than one person, decide whether to pack individual meals or to make packages, each containing one variety of food. Besides all the foregoing ideas under 'Worker' and 'Traveller,' do not forget that green salads pack well in waxed or plastic bags—and remember the salt! Individual flans made in patty-tins instead of a flan-ring are exciting for a car picnic, where they may be carried flat.

A large thermos of ice-cream provides a surprise and much fun.

After your picnic, 'Do gather up your litter from the grass.'

Invalid and Convalescent Cookery

No food requires greater care in the preparation than that for the sick and convalescent, for the feeding of a patient may often help or hinder recovery.

To tempt the appetite it is often a good thing to buy and

prepare small specially suitable delicacies, but in some illnesses it is possible to serve suitable portions from the family meal. In this case the family meal should be planned to fit in with a meal which will be right for the patient, and not vice versa.

The following rules should be followed.

1. Obey the doctor's orders, and if a special diet is necessary see that it is clearly understood and followed.
2. If there are no special restrictions choose food which is easy to digest and which in small bulk will supply the necessary nutriment, especially body-building and body-protecting foods.
3. Food must be fresh and of the best quality. Dairy foods, white fish, white meat, fresh fruit, and vegetables form the basis of most invalid meals.
4. Scrupulous cleanliness throughout preparation, cooking, and serving is necessary.
5. Vary the food in kind, colour, and flavour, always avoiding highly flavoured and highly seasoned foods.
6. Choose suitable methods of cooking, e.g. steaming, avoiding greasiness which is objectionable to taste and also causes food to be indigestible.
7. Taste all foods and drinks to see that they are palatable, and serve hot foods really hot and cold foods quite cold. In cases of serious illness care should be taken not to give drinks too hot, as the patient may not realize that they are too hot to drink.
8. Try to keep the kitchen door closed so that the smell of cooking does not penetrate the house.
9. Serve meals punctually. Often 'a little and often' is a good rule to follow.
10. Always leave a drink to hand, but uneaten food should be taken away at once.
11. Make the tray as attractive as possible—a clean cloth, clean shiny cutlery and glass, pleasing china, a small vase

of flowers. Vary the serving and use little individual
dishes when possible.
12. Give medicine before or after the meal as directed, and do
not leave it near the patient.

DRINKS FOR INVALIDS

When a person is very ill it is necessary to give nourishment
in liquid form so that a drink should often be food as well as
drink. Some of the predigested gruel foods are in this class,
and to make them the instructions on the bottle should be
followed. All milky drinks are in this class. Fruit drinks are
more for refreshment, but if well made can be a valuable
source of vitamin C, and can also supply energy readily if
sweetened with glucose. Clear soups and beef-tea drinks are
not nourishing, but are valuable as stimulants; they have the
effect of making the patient feel able to take a little food, and
consequently a nourishing drink should be given a little later.

BARLEY WATER

2 tablesp. pearl barley.	2 pt. cold water.
½ lemon.	2 teasp. sugar.

To make.

1. Blanch the barley, i.e. wash it thoroughly, put it in a lined
saucepan covered with cold water. Bring it quickly to
the boil, strain, throw away this water.
2. Put the barley back into the saucepan with the 2 pints water
and thinly peeled rind of half a washed lemon.
3. Simmer gently for 1½–2 hours.
4. Strain into a jug. Add the juice of half a lemon and 2
teaspoonfuls sugar.
5. Serve hot or cold.

Note.

If the barley water is to be used to dilute milk, omit all the lemon and
the sugar.

BARLEY WATER FROM BARLEY FLOUR

1 tablesp. prepared barley flour (or fine oatmeal may be
similarly used).
1 pt. boiling water.
A little sugar or salt to taste.

To make.

1. Blend the barley flour with a little cold water.
2. Add 1 pint boiling water, stirring all the time.
3. Return this to the pan and simmer gently 15–20 minutes,
stirring occasionally to prevent sticking.
4. Strain and add a little sugar or salt as desired.

LEMONADE

1 lemon.   1 tablesp. sugar.
1 pt. water.

To make.

1. Wash the lemon and peel off the rind with a potato peeler,
taking care to have no pith.
2. Put the rind, sugar, and ½ pint water in a saucepan and
boil gently to extract colour and flavour.
3. Allow to cool and then strain into a jug.
4. Squeeze the juice from the lemon, and pour this into the
jug through the strainer.
5. Pour the remaining ½ pint water through the strainer, so
rinsing into the jug all the juice and flavour, and making
up the desired quantity.
6. Taste and serve.

LEMONADE MADE WITH GLUCOSE

This supplies energy food.

2 oz. glucose.   2 tablesp. lemon juice.
Rind of 1 lemon.   ¼ pt. water.

To make.

1. Wash the lemon and peel off the rind without pith.

2. Put the water, lemon rind, and glucose in a pan and boil
   gently for 5 minutes.
3. Allow to cool a little. Add the lemon juice.
4. Strain and add more cold water if necessary to make 1
   teacupful.
5. Serve very cold.

BEEF TEA

½ lb. best fresh steak.　　　　pinch of salt.
¾ pt. water.

To make.

1. Wipe the meat, remove all skin and fat.
2. Scrape the meat into shreds and place in a pan.
3. Add water and salt. Cover and stand aside for 30 minutes.
4. Bring very slowly to the boil, almost remove from the heat,
   and continue to simmer very gently for 20 minutes.
5. Remove any fat from the surface by blotting off with a piece
   of clean tissue-paper—or skim carefully off with a spoon.
   Season carefully if permitted.
6. Taste. Serve with fingers of toast.

Note.

Beef tea is often quickly made by stirring 1 teaspoonful Bovril in a cup of
hot water.

EGG FLIP

1 egg.　　　　　　2 teasp. sugar.
½ pt. milk.　　　　1 teasp. brandy if desired.

To make.

1. Remove the speck from the egg, i.e. the stringy bit at the
   join of yolk and white.
2. Add the sugar and beat well.
3. Heat the milk, and when hot, but by no means boiling, pour
   it on to the egg.
4. Stir well. Add brandy if used.
5. Serve in a glass.

Note.

A little sponge cake or a sponge finger biscuit may be served with egg flip.

GRUEL

2 oz. oatmeal.   1 teasp. sugar or pinch of salt.
1 pt. milk.

To make.

1. Soak the oatmeal and milk in a covered basin for 2 hours.
2. Strain.
3. Place the liquid into a lined pan. Stir over gentle heat until boiling. Boil and stir for 5 minutes.
4. Add sugar or salt.
5. Serve hot.

TRAYS FOR CONVALESCENT MEALS

Always put dishes to warm and lay the tray and cover it. Prepare any necessary decoration or garnishes whilst the meal is cooking. Time things so that everything is ready just when you wish it to be. Hot food served on a plate may be covered with an inverted hot basin to keep it hot whilst carrying it upstairs.

AN EXAMPLE OF A DAY'S MEALS FOR A CONVALESCENT

8.30. Breakfast : Half a grape-fruit removed from its skin and served in a dish (see p. 7).
A lightly poached egg on toast.
Toast, butter, and marmalade.
Tea to drink.

10.45. A milk drink and plain biscuit.

12.30. Dinner :   Steamed fish and fish sauce (see p. 80).
*1 tablespoonful mashed potatoes.
1 tablespoonful vegetables—carrots, green peas, cauliflower, kidney beans, etc.
1 baked apple.
Glass of water.

4.0.   Tea :   2 half-slices thinly cut bread and butter.
                   1 Scotch pancake or scone.
                   Jam in a small dish.
                   1 small cake.
                   Tea to drink.

7.0.   Supper :   Tomato soup with fingers of toast (see p. 17).
                   Baked custard (see p. 83).
                   Glass of water.

9.0.   Bedtime
       drink :   Either a hot milk drink or a hot fruit drink.

* *Note.*

   Size of helpings varies with the patient and the illness—the thing to
remember is to try to suit the patient's wishes and appetite.

SUGGESTIONS FOR BREAKFAST

Grape-fruit or cereals or porridge.
Lightly cooked eggs: poached, scrambled, boiled.
Poached haddock, if liked.
Toast, butter, and marmalade, or bread and butter and
   marmalade or honey.
Tea or coffee to drink.

DINNER AND SUPPER DISHES

Steamed fish.   Fish pudding.   Baked fish with tomatoes.
Stewed rabbit, veal, tripe, or liver.
Eggs cooked in different ways, though choose other things if
   eggs are served at breakfast-time.
Light cheese dishes, e.g. cheese pudding.   Macaroni cheese.
Salads.
Cooked chicken.
Soups.
Most fresh vegetables, avoiding any which may cause flatulence,
   e.g. onions, cabbage, dried pulse vegetables.
Puddings—milk, fruit, light sponge puddings, and jellies are
   the best.   Avoid pastry and suet puddings.

The Tea-tray for the Convalescent

Remember to make this as dainty as possible.

Remove the crusts from the bread before making sandwiches, and make these using the thinnest bread and butter you can cut.

Serve small scones cut with a 1-inch cutter.

Make dainty cakes—usually sponge buns or a small piece of jam-filled Victoria Sandwich would be the right type to serve.

Make the tea just before serving, and do not make it strong.

For all meals remember the table-napkin on the tray.

Savoury Dishes suitable for a Convalescent

STEAMED FISH

2 small fillets of plaice.   2 tablesp. milk.
Small piece of margarine.

To make.

1. Skin the fillets, wash, and wipe.
2. Place skinned-side up and head-end towards you on a board. Roll the fillets from head to tail.
3. Tie round with a piece of clean white string.
4. Grease an enamel plate with margarine, pour on 2 table-spoonfuls milk, and stand the rolled fillets on this.
5. Cover with a large pan lid.
6. Place this over a pan of boiling water and steam for about 20 minutes. The plate and contents become hot and the fish steams in its own juices.
7. The fish looks very white and opaque when cooked, and is tender if tested.
8. Pour off the liquid into a $\frac{1}{4}$-pint measure, and leave the

fillets on the plate still covered and over the hot water, though drawn off the heat.

9. Make a roux in a small saucepan, using $\frac{1}{2}$ oz. margarine and $\frac{1}{2}$ oz. flour. Make up the liquor in the measure to $\frac{1}{4}$ pint, using milk. Add this a little at a time to the roux, mixing well with a wooden spoon. When all is added return the pan to gentle heat and stir until boiling. Cook for a minute or two. Season lightly. Taste.

10. Serve the fillets on a hot plate. Coat carefully with a little of the fish sauce. Garnish with two neatly cut lemon butterflies, and a pinch of parsley between the wings (see below). Serve with a small helping of mashed potato, i.e. 1 small tablespoonful, and 1 baked tomato or 1 small tablespoonful of some other cooked vegetable, e.g. carrots, green peas, kidney beans.

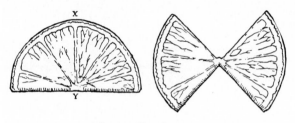

LEMON BUTTERFLIES

Cut the half nearly across from X to Y. Open towards the centre, and place a tiny piece of parsley in the middle.

To cut lemon butterflies.

1. Wash the lemon.
2. Cut in two, parallel to the ends. Remove the pips.
3. Cut a thin ring of lemon about $\frac{1}{8}$ inch thick.
4. Cut this across once.
5. Cut the halves nearly across, beginning at the skin and working to the centre.
6. Open towards the centre. Place a tiny piece of washed parsley in the middle.

POACHED EGG ON SPINACH

To prepare the spinach—cook $\frac{1}{2}$ lb.

1. Remove the stalks except in very young spinach.
2. Wash thoroughly in several waters.
3. Place the washed spinach in a saucepan; the water adhering will be sufficient to start the cooking.
4. Boil for about 15 minutes until tender. Pour into a colander and squeeze the water out, then chop the spinach on a board.
5. Put it back in the pan with a small piece of butter. Reheat carefully.
6. Poach an egg (see *Look and Cook*, p. 72).
7. Make a tidy nest with the spinach on a hot plate and lift the egg carefully into this.
8. Place on the prepared tray. Cover with a hot basin and take to the convalescent.

Sweet Dishes suitable for a Convalescent

EGG CUSTARD

1 egg.	2 drops vanilla essence.
$\frac{3}{4}$ oz. sugar.	$\frac{1}{2}$ pt. milk.

To make.

1. Break the egg. Remove the thread.
2. Add the sugar to the egg and beat together to mix.
3. Pour on the milk and stir together to dissolve the sugar.
4. Strain into a double cooker or into a sufficiently large strong jug, which may be placed in a pan of boiling water to make a substitute 'double cooker.'
5. Stand the double cooker over gentle heat and stir with a wooden spoon all the time until the custard thickens—it will take quite a long time in the jug, but will cook quickly in the true double cooker. In either case watch carefully for signs of thickening, i.e. the custard will coat the back

of the spoon. When this happens lift the custard off the boiling water and pour at once into a cool jug. Stir in the flavouring.

Note.

The egg thickens the milk when they are cooked together. Thickening takes place before boiling point is reached, and if allowed to boil 'curdling' occurs, i.e. the egg becomes lumpy and the liquid thin and watery. A double cooker is used as this regulates the heat, and with careful observation the custard may be made without mishap.

ECONOMICAL EGG CUSTARD

1 egg.	1 heaped tablesp. sugar.
1 heaped dessertsp. cornflour.	1 pt. milk.

4 drops vanilla essence.

To make.

1. Blend the cornflour with a little of the milk.
2. Heat the rest of the milk and sugar.
3. When hot, stir on to the blended cornflour. Return to the pan and stir until boiling.
4. Allow to cool a little.
5. Break the egg, remove the thread, and beat the egg sufficiently to bind it.
6. Stir the egg into the cornflour mixture. Add the flavouring.
7. Stir over gentle heat for a short time to cook the egg without boiling it.

BAKED CUSTARD

1 egg.
1 flat tablesp. sugar.
¼ pt. milk.
2 drops vanilla essence or a little grated nutmeg.

To make.

1. Prepare a moderate oven, and grease with margarine a ½-pint basin or a suitable heatproof dish.
2. Break the egg, remove the thread, beat together the egg and sugar. Stir in the milk.
3. Strain into the dish, taking care to leave no sugar.

4. Grate lightly with nutmeg.
5. Stand in a dripping-tin containing a little water; the water regulates the heat so that the custard sets and does not boil.
6. Bake until set—25–30 minutes.
7. Clean the edge of the dish and serve hot or cold. If a basin is used serve the custard on to a plate or fruit dish.

SPONGE TRIFLE

1 sponge cake (see *Look and Cook*, pp. 128 and 129—make and bake but do not roll).
2 tablesp. raspberry jam, or ½ lb. stewed apple, or some tinned fruit.
½ pt. custard (see p. 82).

To make.

1. Polish a glass fruit dish or four individual dishes.
2. Cut the cake into 1-inch squares and arrange in the dish with the jam sandwiched between the pieces or with the fruit arranged on top and the juice poured over.
3. Pour over the custard and leave for 1 hour before serving so that the juices and custard can soak the sponge cake.
4. Decorate the top with one or two blanched almonds and glacé cherries.

INVALID JELLY

1 lemon.	¼ pt. water.
1 orange.	2½ oz. lump sugar.
¼ oz. gelatine or 1 rounded teasp.	1 fresh egg.

To make.

1. Have ready three or four small aluminium moulds or small Pyrex cups or other suitable individual shapes.
2. Wash the fruit. Rub the rinds with the lumps of sugar.
3. Place the sugar, water, and gelatine in a saucepan and stir over very gentle heat to melt the gelatine. Bring slowly to the boil.
4. Squeeze the juice from the fruit, and if necessary make up with water to measure ⅛ pint, i.e. 4 tablespoonfuls.

5. Add the ⅛ pint juice to the gelatine mixture.
6. Break the egg, beat it, and stir the gelatine mixture on to it.   Mix well.
7. Strain into a jug.   Taste.
8. Fill the moulds with the jelly.
9. Stand in a cold place to set—2 hours (a shorter time in a refrigerator).
10. Turn out.

To turn out a jelly.

Dip quickly into a deep basin of fairly hot water—blot with a tea-towel to remove water from the jelly top and the sides of the mould.   Invert on a shiny plate.

HONEYCOMB MOULD

2 eggs.	4 drops vanilla essence.
½ pt. milk.	Short ½ oz. gelatine or 2 small teasp.
1 oz. sugar.	2 tablesp. water.

To make.

1. Have ready a 1½-pint mould.
2. Separate the yolks from the whites of the eggs.
3. Make a custard with the beaten yolks, sugar, and milk (see p. 82).   Add vanilla essence.
4. Dissolve the gelatine in the water in a small pan over very gentle heat.   Stir well.
5. Add the gelatine to the custard and mix.   Allow to cool a little.
6. Whisk the egg whites stiffly and fold into the custard mixture.
7. Pour into the mould and turn out when set.

BLACKCURRANT PURÉE

This may be bought in tins or bottles, and is rich in vitamin C, and is therefore useful in invalid and convalescent drinks.   It may also be served with ground rice or semolina puddings, with blancmange or with junket.

Meals for Toddlers and Young Children

From about six months old young babies are introduced to
a few semi-solid foods in addition to milk. This change is
carried out gradually, following some of the excellent leaflets
and charts available.

When children have sufficient teeth to chew fairly hard
foods they are introduced to the ordinary family meals. This
is a very important time in their training and is also a time of
gradual change.

GENERAL RULES FOR FEEDING CHILDREN

1. The meals must be carefully balanced to include the nutri-
   ents which are most important for children. Children
   need plenty of the body-building foods to make them
   grow. They need milk for their teeth and bones, vegetables and fruits to protect them from illness. All these
   are more important for children than the energy foods
   (see *Look and Cook*, 'Right Feeding for Health,' p. 8).
2. Children's meals should be punctual and regular, day by
   day and week by week. This helps to ensure good food
   habits from the beginning.
3. Introduce foods to give bite, such as rusks and crusts, and
   as much colour and as great a variety of foods as possible.
4. Even hungry children have small capacities, so do not fill
   them up with too much liquid or with big helpings of
   bread or potato until they have eaten the more important
   foods. Never overload their plates; let them ask for
   more if still hungry. Begin very young children with
   quite a small spoonful of meat, vegetable, and potato,
   and increase the quantities as they become older.
5. Most children under five need their food cut up a little.
   This applies especially to meat, bacon, fried bread, and
   other hard foods. Care should be taken to remove all
   bones, gristle, and hard skins. Many children find the

concentration needed for feeding themselves very tiring, and although still hungry they cannot make the effort to eat. These children should be given a little help from time to time before they become too tired to finish the meal.

6. Aim at a peaceful, happy atmosphere at meal-times. Time spent in training children to eat the right foods in the right way is well worth while.

THE TABLE

1. Give very young children two teaspoons, and then let them progress to a small fork and one teaspoon.
2. Children need definite teaching on how to use a knife and fork; they should be able to manage a small knife and fork comfortably by the time they are five years old.
3. Use suitable dishes so that the food is not spilled. Small deep dishes are the most suitable for children.
4. Accidental spills should not matter too much. Use a special plastic mat or old cloth for the table, and save unnecessary washing by using feeders and pinafores.
5. Avoid giving children very hot or over-seasoned foods. Food should be well moistened, but do not give too much gravy or sauce.
6. Have the chair the right height for the child to sit up straight, but comfortably in reach of the table. Make quite sure that high chairs are safe. A strong active child is better on an ordinary chair with a cushion or a special low chair with its own tray.

SUGGESTIONS FOR MEALS FOR A TODDLER FOR ONE DAY

Quantities are suitable for a three-year-old. A little less or more is given to those younger or older.

Before breakfast: Half a glass of orange juice and water, or rose-hip syrup and water. If breakfast is some time after the children wake they may need a

D

biscuit or a slice of bread and butter, but this should be avoided if possible.

Breakfast: 1–2 tablespoonfuls porridge or cereals.   Sugar or syrup and milk poured over.

⅓ rasher bacon.   ½ slice fried bread.

½ to 1 slice bread and butter or rusks or toast with honey.

Milk to drink.

Mid-morning: A milky drink.   A piece of apple or raw carrot to chew.

Dinner: 1 tablespoonful chopped liver and gravy.

1 tablespoonful cabbage or carrot.

1 tablespoonful baked potato.

1½ tablespoonfuls blackcurrant fool with 1 sweet biscuit.

Water to drink.

Tea: 1 or 2 slices brown bread and butter and jam.

A small sponge bun.

A sweet biscuit.

Milk to drink.

Before bed: Milk and biscuits if desired.

Sweets: Choose good quality sweets for young children, and give them two or three a day.   After meals is the best time.

OTHER FOODS SUITABLE FOR YOUNG CHILDREN

Breakfast: Coddled egg.   Scrambled egg.   Boiled egg.   Herring roes.   Creamed haddock.

Dinner: Lean meat.   Boned fish.   Small pieces of rabbit taken off the bone.   Liver should be served as often as possible.   Egg custard.   Milk puddings. Sponge puddings.   Fresh fruit puddings.

Teas: Sandwiches.   Watercress.

Junket or blancmange.

The meals for each day should be chosen to fit in with each other. A more substantial tea may be served after a light dinner.

As the children become older they will need more substantial meals. Care must be taken to give children all the necessary body-building and protective foods during the whole time they are growing.

MILK

Children under five years should have at least 1 pint of milk daily. Many children are able to drink this quantity, but some children will need their daily milk allowance in other forms.

Milky drinks: Ovaltine, Horlicks, cocoa, Bournvita.
Sauces: White sauce with fish or rabbit. Custard sauce.
Puddings: Blancmange, egg custard, junket, rice puddings, semolina, or ground rice pudding served with rose-hip syrup or blackcurrant purée.

Vary the shape, colour, and flavouring of milk puddings. During the winter supplementary vitamin foods are often recommended for children—cod-liver oil, rose-hip syrup, or orange juice.

RUSKS

These are crisp, and may be served instead of bread and butter. They help to encourage the change from soft foods to a mixed diet.

1 slice of bread.

To make.

1. Cut the bread $\frac{1}{2}$ inch thick. Cut it into three fingers.
2. Bake in a cool oven until pale golden brown and crisp through.
3. Serve with butter and Marmite, honey or jam.

Note.

Several slices of bread may be made into rusks at once if they are kept crisp in an air-tight tin.

SWEET RUSKS

1 slice of bread.
1 tablesp. of made cocoa, sweetened, or
1 teasp. honey or jam dissolved in 1 tablesp. warm water.

To make.

1. Cut the bread ½ inch thick and cut into neat fingers.
2. Prepare the cocoa or dissolve the honey or jam.
3. Dip the bread in the sweet liquid.
4. Dry in a cool oven until quite crisp and golden brown.
5. To prevent sticking to the baking-tray turn the rusks over occasionally as they dry.

Note.

Other milky drinks or sweet liquids may be used for dipping the bread.

CODDLED EGG

1 fresh egg.

This is a very lightly boiled egg in the most digestible form.

To cook.

1. Half fill a saucepan with water and bring to the boil.
2. Lower the egg carefully into the boiling water.
3. Draw the pan off the heat and cover with a lid.
4. Allow the egg 5–6 minutes to cook.
5. Serve as for boiled egg.

STEWED LIVER
(One or two helpings)

2 oz. liver.	½ carrot.	A piece of celery.
Few scraps of bacon.	¼ onion.	1 rounded teasp. flour.
¼ pt. stock or water.	Seasoning.	

To cook.

1. Prepare the vegetables and cut into neat dice or slices.
2. Wash the liver, remove any coarse pieces, and cut into small thin slices.
3. Cut off the bacon rinds and cut the bacon up into pieces.

4. Fry the bacon in a small pan until crisp. Add the vegetables, and fry slowly to develop a good flavour. Shake frequently and do not allow to stick. The bacon fat should be sufficient, but a little dripping may be added if necessary.

5. Add the liver, stock, and seasoning. Bring to the boil, then reduce the heat and allow the stew to simmer. Allow about 30–40 minutes.

6. Blend the flour to a smooth cream with a little cold water, about 3 teaspoonfuls.

7. Test the liver and vegetables with a skewer, and when tender stir in the blended flour. Stir and cook for 3 minutes. Add a little gravy browning if necessary, taste, season, and serve. The gravy should be just thick enough to coat the liver smoothly.

Note.

1. This length of time is suitable for ox liver, but calves' or lambs' liver, which is more tender, will not take so long.

2. Allow $\frac{1}{2}$–$\frac{3}{4}$ lb. liver and 2 rashers of bacon if stewing liver for 4 or 5 people.

Children's Parties

For successful children's parties good planning is essential. Cakes and biscuits should be baked a few days before the party to allow time for the trimmings and decorations that make them into party fare.

Children's parties are usually birthday or Christmas parties, and the food chosen should suit the occasion.

GENERAL RULES

1. Consider the age and number of the children.

2. Plan carefully, thinking of the space, help, and time available.

3. Judge the quantities required accurately. Do not give small children big helpings at first.

4. The best party fare is simple familiar food, which is served or arranged differently. Avoid all rich indigestible food, omit pastries and too many rich, cream-filled cakes.

5. Arrange the table so that the children are attracted at first sight. Make it colourful and fresh. Make sure that nothing can be knocked over and that the children are seated comfortably. Children like to have their places named with individual cards.

The order of serving the party tea varies. Some people prefer to begin with jelly or blancmange, whilst others prefer to have them later.

A birthday cake is put in the centre of the table, and is eaten last. It is usual to include some food from each of the following groups:

1. Jelly. Blancmange. Fruit salad. Trifle. Ice-cream.
2. Bread and butter. Sandwiches. Small tea scones.
3. Biscuits: plain, fancy shapes, iced, chocolate.
4. Small cakes, plain, iced.
5. Large cakes, including birthday cakes.
6. Drinks: tea, milk, lemonade, orangeade.

Recipes for blancmange, fruit salad, plain scones, biscuits, and cakes will be found in *Look and Cook*. Many other suggestions suitable for a party tea will be found in the section on teas, p. 43, and the trifle given on p. 84 may also be adapted for a party.

ORANGE JELLIES

Buy a good quality packet jelly, and follow the instructions on the packet carefully.

Jellies may be set in a large mould or individual dishes, or an attractive way of serving jelly for children is in fresh orange skins.

1 pt. packet of jelly.   4 oranges.

To make.

1. Dissolve the jelly, leave to cool.
2. Wash the oranges, cut across in two. Using a teaspoon scoop out the flesh and juice without damaging the skins. The orange may be used for orangeade, fruit salad, or eaten by the family.
3. Use a pair of scissors and vandyke the edges of the orange skins to decorate. If desired, narrow, semicircular handles can be cut from a spare half-orange skin (see diagram).
4. When the jelly is cool fill the prepared orange skins, stand together on a plate, and leave in a cool place to set. The handles are arranged over the orange jellies before serving.

1. Prepare empty half-orange skin. Vandyke the edge with a pair of scissors.

2. The orange-skin basket filled with jelly and with an orange-peel handle.

To prepare an Orange-skin Basket

Note.

1. Jellies may be set in individual dishes and a layer of custard or blancmange poured over when the jelly is firm. When the custard is cold decorate with funny faces by using currants and pieces of cherry.
2. Two colours of jelly may be made; set one colour in the dishes and pour the second jelly over when it is quite cold but still liquid.
3. Bananas may be sliced and put into the dishes before the jelly is poured in.

BISCUITS

Fancy home-made biscuits are always very popular at a party. Make ½ lb. plain biscuit mixture and finish in various ways.

½ lb. flour.	4 oz. sugar.
Pinch of salt.	4 oz. margarine.
¼ teasp. baking-powder.	½ egg.

To make.

1. Prepare a moderate oven. Grease a baking-tray.
2. Sieve the flour, salt, and baking-powder together.
3. Cream the sugar and fat together until light and smooth.
4. Add the ½ egg. Beat an egg well to halve evenly.
5. Stir in the flour, and work together with a wooden spoon until it is even. The mixture must be stiff enough to cut out.
6. Roll out thinly and cut into the desired shapes. Place on a baking-tray and bake until a light golden colour—15–20 minutes. Allow biscuits to set a little before lifting on to a cooling-tray.

SHAPES AND DECORATIONS

1. *Animals and little men.*

There are many fancy cutters available in the form of little men, ducks, rabbits, teddy bears, and dogs. Put a small currant or piece of date to make the eyes.

These biscuits may be left plain or iced with glacé icing.

2. *Traffic Light Biscuits.*

    (*a*) Roll the biscuit mixture about ⅛ inch thick.

    (*b*) Make a pattern from a plain postcard of a rectangle 3 inches by 1 inch. Use this to cut neat, accurate biscuits.

    (*c*) Put half the biscuits upside-down on a greased baking-tray.

(d) Use a very small plain round cutter or a well-washed thimble. Cut three circles out of the remaining biscuits in a straight line. Be sure to allow a margin all round and between the holes.

(e) Damp the edges of the biscuits already on the tray. Place the cut biscuits right side up on top of them.

(f) Bake in a moderate oven for 15–20 minutes until an even golden colour. When cooked lift on to a cooling-tray.

(g) Prepare the coloured filling. Keep separate in three small basins.

> 1 tablesp. red jam, brightened with a drop of red colouring if necessary.
> 1 tablesp. lemon curd or sieved marmalade or apricot jam.
> 1 tablesp. lemon curd or apricot jam coloured green.

(h) When the biscuits are cool dredge with a little icing sugar.

(j) Put in just sufficient of each colour jam to fill the holes. Remember to keep to the correct sequence. Red, amber, green.

(k) Arrange neatly on a plate.

ICED BISCUITS

1. Bake a selection of different shaped biscuits.
2. Mix 4 oz. glacé icing (see p. 53).
3. Prepare small pieces of glacé cherry, nuts, or pieces of orange or lemon rind for decoration.
4. Use a teaspoon and coat the surface of the biscuits evenly. Decorate lightly.
5. The icing may be of different colours and flavours.

*D

FEATHER-ICED BISCUITS

1. Follow the instructions given for feather-iced sandwich cake on p. 53.
2. Use a small paper bag with the point cut off to allow a very small line of icing to run through. Keep the lines close together.
3. The contrasting colour should be definite. Chocolate on white icing or white on chocolate icing is popular with children.

NAMED BISCUITS

1. Cut the biscuits into neat rectangles, and bake.
2. Cover with plain white or pink icing.
3. When set use a bag either with a writing pipe or as for feather icing, and one or two teaspoonfuls of a contrasting colour of glacé icing.
4. Print or write the children's names on the biscuits.

Note.

Domino biscuits may be made by piping spots instead of names.

Cakes

CHOCOLATE LOG

This is always a popular cake, but is particularly suitable for a Christmas party.

Swiss Roll

2 eggs.	2 oz. flour.
3 oz. sugar.	½ teasp. baking-powder.

Butter Icing

2 oz. margarine.	Few drops vanilla essence.
3 oz. icing sugar.	1 dessertsp. milk.

1 tablesp. chocolate powder and 1 dessertsp. cocoa.

Decorations

A spray of holly and a Father Christmas or robin.

To make.

1. Make the Swiss roll. (See *Look and Cook*, p. 129.) Roll up without jam and leave until cold.

2. Cream the margarine and sugar together until very white and fluffy. Add the vanilla essence, chocolate powder, and cocoa. Beat the icing until smooth and evenly coloured. Add sufficient milk to make a soft cream that will spread easily.

3. Unroll the Swiss roll and spread about a quarter of the butter icing thinly over the surface. Roll up carefully.

4. Trim about 3 inches off the end of the roll, making a slanting cut. Fix the piece cut off at an angle to the main roll to make a small branch. A little jam or some of the icing is used for this.

5. Spread the rest of the butter icing thinly over the top and sides of the roll and branch. Leave the ends free. Let the icing spread down as far as the plate.

6. Draw a fork lightly through the butter icing. This represents the bark of the tree.

7. Lightly dredge the top with icing sugar to represent snow.

8. Decorate the log with a Father Christmas, spray of holly, or a robin.

A BIRTHDAY LAYER CAKE

The Cake	*The Filling*
6 oz. margarine.	2 oz. margarine.
6 oz. castor sugar.	3 oz. icing sugar.
3 eggs.	Flavouring.
6 oz. flour.	*Glacé Icing*
1 rounded teasp. baking-powder.	4 oz. icing sugar.
A little milk.	3–4 teasp. warm water or fruit juice.

To Decorate

Candle holders. Candles. Coco-nut.

To make.

1. Prepare and bake the cake as for Victoria Sandwich (see p. 51), using three 6- or 7-inch sandwich-tins.

2. Cream the margarine and icing sugar until white and fluffy. Add the milk or cream to give a soft consistency. Colour and flavour as desired.

3. Spread the butter icing on top of two of the cakes and sandwich the three cakes together.

4. Make the glacé icing. Put a paper collar round the cake (see p. 125), and spread the glacé icing evenly over the surface.

5. When ready arrange the candle holders with candles on top and finish with a neat circle of coco-nut sprinkled over the edge of the icing.

Note.

1. Before beginning to make the cake, decide upon the colour and flavour of the cake. This usually depends on the colour of the candles and holders.

2. Butter icing may be left plain, flavoured with vanilla, made into coffee or chocolate icing, or flavoured with grated orange rind.

3. Glacé icing is best left white with brightly coloured candles, or it may be chocolate, coffee, pink, or orange.

4. The coco-nut may be left white or coloured by rubbing well with a few drops of colouring. Do this with a teaspoon in a basin or between the hands over a paper.

Vegetarian Meals

Vegetarians do not eat meat, fish, or bacon, and products containing these things, e.g. Bovril, meat dripping, and fish paste. This means that main dishes are usually made up of milk, cheese, or eggs.

General Points

1. Owing to the limited choice of body-building foods care must be taken to include sufficient of the foods allowed.

2. Meat and fish juices have very particular flavours which

increase the appetite and help with digestion. Without these juices the foods may become monotonous or insipid, therefore it is important to use other strongly flavoured foods, e.g. celery, onions, Marmite, spices, herbs, curry powder.

3. Because fruits and vegetables are often very expensive, fruits should be preserved when cheapest, that is, in season, in as large quantities as possible.

4. Introduce variety into the meals, and serve plenty of salads.

5. Health stores sell many special vegetarian preparations and fats made from vegetable oils which are used for making pastry and for frying.

6. It is usual to serve potatoes and two other vegetables for a vegetarian dinner. By serving dried or fresh peas and beans the body-building content of the dinner is increased.

SUGGESTIONS FOR VEGETARIAN MEALS

Many well-known dishes are suitable for serving to vegetarians, but care must be taken to adapt the recipes correctly, e.g. lentil soup (see *Look and Cook*, p. 50) and tomato soup on p. 17. Omit the bone and bacon rind and use vegetable water for stock and vegetable fat for dripping.

Most of the familiar puddings and sweet dishes are suitable if vegetable fat is used. Lard and suet must not be used, but most puddings are successful if these are replaced with vegetable fat.

MAIN DISHES

Macaroni cheese (*Look and Cook*, p. 75).   Cheese eggs (p. 34).
Cheese pudding (*Look and Cook*, p. 76).   Cauliflower cheese (p. 34).
Savoury omelets (p. 68).

CURRIED EGGS

4 hard-boiled eggs.   Curry sauce (p. 26, Nos. 1–4).
3 oz. boiled rice (p. 26).

To make.

1. Prepare a well-flavoured curry sauce as described on p. 26, Nos. 1–4. Use vegetable fat for dripping.
2. Boil and dry the rice as described on p. 26.
3. Hard-boil four eggs. Remove the shells and cut the eggs lengthways in half. Arrange cut side down in a hot deep dish. Keep warm.
4. When the sauce is ready taste, season, and pour over and round the eggs. Arrange the dried rice round the edge, and garnish with chopped parsley.

Note.

Alternatively the eggs may be cut up into large pieces and warmed through in the curry sauce.

CURRIED VEGETABLES

2 lb. mixed vegetables (include soaked pulse vegetables if possible).
Curry sauce (p. 26, Nos. 1–4). Rice (p. 26).

To make.

1. Prepare the curry sauce as described on p. 26. Use vegetable fat for dripping.
2. Boil and dry the rice (p. 26).
3. Prepare and cut up the vegetables. Large dice or thick slices are best. The vegetables should be easy to eat, but must keep their shape during cooking.
4. Add the vegetables to the curry, and allow to simmer until quite tender, 30–40 minutes.
5. Serve in a hot deep dish, and arrange the rice round the edge. Garnish with chopped parsley.

Note.

If dried peas or beans are used they should be partly cooked first. Lentils may be used without previous cooking.

TO COOK HARICOT BEANS, BUTTER BEANS, AND DRIED PEAS

Peas and beans are known as pulse vegetables. They should be included in mixed vegetable dishes for vegetarians as they add to the body-building content of the meal.

Lentils may be cooked as described below, or they may be cooked without preliminary soaking.

Allow ½ lb. dried pulse vegetables for four people.

To cook.

1. Think of this vegetable the day before. Wash thoroughly. Put in a large mixing bowl, add 1 teaspoonful bicarbonate of soda, cover with boiling water, and leave to soak overnight.
2. Next day pour off the water and wash again.
3. Put the soaked vegetables in a pan, cover with cold water, and bring slowly to the boil. (Omit the salt until later.)
4. Boil gently 2½–3 hours until they are quite tender. Dried vegetables must not be served until they are thoroughly soft. Fill up the pan with more boiling water if necessary.
5. Drain off the water, add salt and pepper, and a small piece of margarine. Shake in the pan to mix the seasoning evenly.
6. Serve neatly in a hot vegetable dish and garnish with a sprig of parsley.

VEGETABLE HOT-POT and VEGETABLE PIE

These may be made as for meat hot-pot and meat pie. Use a variety of vegetables in season, include a few partly cooked pulse vegetables if possible, and add herbs and seasoning to give a good flavour.

Vegetable pie can be made with short crust pastry, potato pastry (see p. 65), or mashed potatoes as in shepherd's pie.

Cooked vegetable dishes should be eaten the day they are made.

SAVOURY RICE

4 oz. rice.	1 level teasp. mixed herbs
1 onion.	(parsley, thyme, marjoram).
2 oz. vegetable fat.	2 tomatoes.
1 pt. vegetable stock.	3 oz. grated cheese.
Salt and pepper.	

To make.

1. Melt the fat, chop the onion, wash the rice.
2. Add the rice and onion to the hot fat and fry together without browning for 5 minutes.
3. Add the stock, use water and ¼ teaspoonful Marmite if no vegetable stock. Add the seasoning and chopped herbs.
4. Simmer slowly until the rice is cooked. Squeeze a grain between thumb and finger to test.
5. Skin the tomato by dipping quickly into boiling water. Cut into small pieces and add to the rice, add the grated cheese, and stir to prevent sticking. The liquid should be almost absorbed and the mixture hot, savoury, and creamy.
6. Serve in a hot deep dish and garnish with a sprig of parsley.

INDIVIDUAL SALADS

Salads which are put ready on individual plates make attractive light meals, and can be served all the year round. Use a variety of ingredients, and serve with brown bread and butter or baked potatoes.

Choose ingredients from among the following groups:

1. Lettuce, watercress, shredded cabbage, or Brussels sprouts, mustard and cress.
2. Beetroot, grated carrot, grated swede, celery.
3. Tomatoes, radish, spring onions.
4. Sliced orange, apple, banana, raisins, dates.
5. Walnuts, coco-nut, almonds.
6. Cheese, eggs.
7. Salad dressing or lemon juice.

To prepare.

1. Wash and prepare all the vegetables according to kind (see *Look and Cook*, pp. 15–28).
2. Shred and grate the vegetables just before serving to prevent loss of vitamin C.
3. Tomatoes may be sliced or quartered. Wash well and skin if necessary.

4. Slice oranges and bananas. Apples are better if cut into dice. Lemon juice squeezed over the apple will prevent browning.
5. Nuts are chopped and mixed with other ingredients or served separately.
6. Cheese is cut into neat cubes, grated, or made into a cream with a little milk. Eggs are sliced or cut in halves.
7. An uncooked or a cooked salad dressing is always served with salad to add moisture and piquancy. Lemon juice is used as a substitute if people do not like vinegar. Serve the dressing separately in a bottle or sauce-boat.
8. Mixtures of peas and cooked diced vegetables can be blended together with 2 or 3 teaspoonfuls of salad dressing. Mix very lightly to avoid breaking up the dice.

To serve.

1. Arrange the salad on individual plates according to the size of the salad to be served.
2. Leave a space for the potato.
3. Arrange the salad lightly and neatly. Include a little of everything prepared. Keep the ingredients in small groups, avoid mixing together too much. Lettuce leaves are prettier if left whole.

CHEESE BALLS FOR THE SALAD

4 tablesp. grated cheese.	Salt and pepper.
A pinch of mustard.	Coco-nut or chopped nuts.
A little milk.	

To make.

1. Prepare the cheese, add the seasonings.
2. Mix the cheese with a little milk until it is a stiff but moist consistency.
3. Roll small heaps of the cheese into balls, about eight.
4. Roll each ball in the coco-nut or chopped nuts until evenly coated. Keep a good shape.

Note.

Crushed cornflakes make an attractive golden coating for cheese balls.

STUFFED TOMATOES

4 firm, even-sized tomatoes.	1 teasp. chopped shallot or onion.
4 teasp. grated cheese.	½ oz. margarine.
2 tablesp. fresh breadcrumbs.	1 teasp. chopped parsley.

Salt and pepper.

To cook.

1. Wash the tomatoes. Mark the opposite end from the stalk with a small round cutter. Use a vegetable knife and cut neatly round this mark to lift off a lid. Keep the lids carefully on a plate.

2. Use the handle of a teaspoon and scoop out the pulp juice from the inside of the tomato. Keep the pulp in a basin.

3. Prepare the breadcrumbs, grated cheese, chopped parsley, and onion.

4. Melt the margarine, add the onion, and fry slowly until the onion is quite cooked; avoid browning too much. Add the rest of the ingredients, the seasoning, and the tomato pulp.

5. Put the mixture evenly into the prepared tomatoes, using a teaspoon. Place the tomato lid on top of the filling so that it is a little raised above the tomato.

6. Garnish with parsley or watercress, and serve cold with a salad or on rounds of brown bread and butter.

7. The remainder of the stuffing should be rolled into balls and served with the salad or spread on fingers of toast spread with Marmite.

Note.

Stuffed tomatoes may be baked in a moderate oven until tender and served hot, on pieces of fried bread. Extra stuffing may also be baked and served on fried bread.

Other fillings may be used, chopped cooked mushrooms or cooked diced vegetables.

3

TRADITIONAL FARE AND LOCAL DISHES

Traditional Cookery

TRADITIONAL cookery in our own and other lands is a fascinating study. It is usual to commemorate outstanding days with special cookery, and interesting when travelling to sample the food which is special to the particular locality. This chapter can only suggest a few of these recipes, but aims also to encourage the reader to find out more about these specialities and to practise making things which have become traditional because they are valued by the generations of people in the district from which they come.

SEASONAL FARE FOLLOWING THE CALENDAR

Shrove Tuesday.

PANCAKES
(Makes four large or six small pancakes)

4 oz. flour.	1 egg.
Pinch of salt.	½ pt. milk.

These are the ingredients for Yorkshire pudding batter, and often the batter is made in the usual way as described in *Look and Cook*, pp. 98 and 99. Lighter pancakes, though a little more difficult to fry, may be made in the following way:

To make.

1. Sieve together the flour and salt.
2. Separate the yolk from the white of the egg, and save the white on a plate.
3. Make a well in the centre of the flour and drop in the yolk.
4. Gradually mix in the milk, using a wooden spoon, until rather more than half of it is added. At the same time

stir in the flour until it is all mixed down from the sides of the bowl, and a thick creamy consistency is obtained.

5. Beat well for 3–4 minutes.

6. Stir in the rest of the milk.

7. Cover and leave to stand in a cold place.

8. Just before frying whisk up the white of egg stiffly. This may be done on a plate using a knife or in a large bowl using a whisk. A pinch of salt added helps the process.

9. When nothing but froth and so stiff that the white of egg may be drawn up in stiff points, cut and fold this into the batter.

10. Make a small piece of lard hot in the frying-pan. Tilt the pan so that all the bottom is greased, and wait until the fat is slightly smoking.

11. Using a tea-cup or gill measure pour in sufficient batter to cover the bottom of the pan when tilted.

12. Fry quickly, moving the pan on the heat if necessary to ensure even frying.

13. Loosen the edges of the pancake, and shake from time to time to keep the bottom loose.

14. When golden beneath toss with a flick of the wrist. If inexperienced try over the table or turn with a palette knife.

15. Fry the other side similarly.

16. Turn on to a sugared paper, sprinkle with lemon or orange juice and sugar, and roll up.

17. Place on a hot dish and keep hot until the others are fried (repeating instructions 10–17), then serve at once with pieces of lemon or orange, and extra sugar in a basin.

For Mothering Sunday (Mid Lent).   A cake for a girl to give to her mother.

SIMNEL CAKE

SIMNEL CAKE

5½ oz. margarine.	3 eggs.
5 oz. castor sugar.	½ lb. currants.
5½ oz. flour.	2 oz. candied peel.
½ teasp. baking-powder.	

Almond Paste

4 oz. ground almonds.	3 drops almond essence.
7 oz. castor sugar.	Beaten egg to mix.

To make.

1. Line a 7-inch cake-tin with double greased greaseproof paper.
2. Draw round the bottom of the tin on paper for a pattern.
3. Set the oven at Regulo 6 or 400° F.
4. Make the almond paste:
   (*a*) Mix the ground almonds and sugar.
   (*b*) Add the almond essence, and carefully mix with

beaten egg to obtain a stiff consistency. Knead well—the paste should be pliable and not crumbly.

(c) Cut off a piece as big as a walnut, and wrap this in greaseproof paper to make into birds' eggs.

(d) Divide the rest in two.

(e) Roll half into a round, slightly smaller than the pattern of the bottom of the tin.

(f) Make the other piece into a sausage shape, and divide into 16 equal pieces. Roll these in the hand into balls, which when placed together on the pattern of the tin should just touch each other. Flatten slightly to make them close up if necessary. Do this on the pattern. Save until the cake is baked.

5. Make the cake as for rich cake mixture (see *Look and Cook*, p. 124), mixing to a soft, dropping consistency.

6. Spread half the cake mixture in the tin. Make level.

7. Place the flat circle of almond mixture on this layer of cake mixture, and press gently to make it flat.

8. Spread the remaining half of the cake mixture on top, making a very small well in the centre—about 2 inches across and $\frac{1}{2}$ inch deep.

9. See that apart from the well the top is quite level.

10. Bake just above the centre of the oven.

11. After 10 minutes, without looking, reduce the oven heat to Regulo 3 or 300° F. Look carefully after an hour, and regulate the heat if necessary after this.

12. Bake for about $2\frac{1}{4}$ hours, until the cake is evenly golden brown, and firm to the touch in the centre, or if tested with a fine skewer this comes out without a trace of mixture adhering.

13. Lift the tin on to a pan-stand on the table.

14. Brush round the top edge of the cake with the egg left from the almond paste, and stick the balls of almond side by side round the top (see photograph, p. 109). Put

a small round of margarine paper on the cake to prevent further browning.

15. Turn up the oven heat to Regulo 6 or 400° F., and put the cake back to bake the balls till golden in colour. Watch this process carefully, as it will not take long, and it may be necessary to turn the cake round to get them even in colour.

16. Take the cake from the oven. Allow to cool a little, then lift from the tin to a cooling-tray. When cold, store in a cake-tin.

To decorate the Simnel cake.

1. Make little birds' eggs with the remaining piece of almond paste. Paint and speckle these with icing colourings, making blackbirds', robins', thrushes' eggs, etc.

2. Allow the colours to dry.

3. When dry prepare white glacé icing as follows: Mix 4 tablespoonfuls of sieved icing sugar with a little warmed water. This should be added from a teaspoon to produce a coating consistency.

4. Carefully pour this glacé icing on to the top of the cake, and with a knife help it to fill in the scallops made by the almond balls.

5. Place the eggs where you would like them.

For Good Friday.

HOT CROSS BUNS

½ lb. flour.	1 egg.
1 oz. lard or margarine.	⅛ pt. warm milk.
¾ oz. yeast. ⎫	1½ oz. sugar.
½ teasp. sugar. ⎭	1 oz. currants.
½ teasp. salt.	¾ teasp. spice.
½ oz. peel.	

To make.

Remember to keep the dough warm and free from draughts so that light buns result.

1. Sieve the flour and salt into a warm bowl.
2. Rub in the fat.
3. Make a well in the flour and pour in the yeast creamed with 1 level teaspoonful sugar.
4. Beat the egg, and pour this on to the yeast.
5. Warm the milk, and when tepid pour this in.
6. Cover and set to sponge in a warm place.
7. Clean the currants, chop the peel, and put these with the sugar and spice.
8. When sponged, have ready a little more tepid milk and mix the dough with a wooden spoon. A light dough is required, i.e. it must not be stiff and dry, but pliable and rather sticky at first. A little of the extra milk may be required to obtain this consistency.
9. Beat well with the spoon or with the hand. When the outside of the dough is smooth add the fruit, spice, and sugar. Mix well, then beat the dough until it is completely mixed, i.e. no traces of spice or sugar may be seen.
10. Cover. Wrap up in a clean tea-cloth or double newspaper, and put to rise in a warm place.
11. After 1 hour or more, when the dough has doubled its size, shape the buns.
12. Have ready a warm greased baking-tray and a fairly hot oven.
13. Lift the dough on to a lightly floured board, toss in the flour to prevent sticking, then knead lightly.
14. Cut into eight pieces.
15. Knead each into a round, roll a little, and place on the tin.
16. Mark a cross on top with a knife, or make a cross with small strips of pastry. Damp these, and place in position.

17. Prove 15–20 minutes.   Prepare glaze (see below).
18. Bake above the centre of the oven until well risen, gold and firm round the edges.
19. Brush with glaze and return to the oven for 2 or 3 minutes.
20. Lift from the tin to a cooling-tray.

Glaze.

Mix 2 teaspoonfuls sugar with 1 tablespoonful milk, and stir over gentle heat until slightly thick.   Thin glaze soaks into the buns and spoils them.

EASTER BISCUITS

3 oz. margarine.	6 oz. flour.
3 oz. castor sugar.	Pinch of salt.
1 egg yolk or $\frac{1}{2}$ a beaten egg with a little milk if necessary.	$\frac{1}{2}$ oz. chopped peel.
	1 oz. currants.
$\frac{1}{4}$ teasp. spice (if liked).	

To make.

1. Prepare a moderate oven.   Grease a baking-tray.
2. Cream the margarine and sugar.
3. Mix together the flour, salt, chopped peel, and cleaned currants and spice if used.
4. Beat the egg and mix in the egg and dry ingredients, adding alternately.
5. Add very little milk if required to mix to a firm dough.
6. Roll out $\frac{1}{4}$ inch thick on a lightly floured board.
7. Prick all over.
8. Cut out, using a 3-inch cutter.   Place on the tin.   Bake carefully until golden brown.
9. Lift at once to a cooling-tray.   If the biscuits round the edge of the tin are ready first, lift these, and leave the rest a little longer.

Hallowe'en and Bonfire Fare.

YORKSHIRE PARKIN

6 oz. flour.	1 teasp. baking-powder.
6 oz. medium oatmeal.	½ teasp. bicarbonate of soda.
2 oz. Demerara sugar.	8 oz. treacle or syrup.
1 teasp. ginger.	½ pt. milk.

3 oz. lard or margarine.

To make.

1. Prepare a very moderate oven.
2. Grease a Yorkshire-pudding tin and line the bottom with greased greaseproof paper.
3. Crush out the lumps from the bicarbonate of soda, and then mix together all the dry ingredients.
4. Place the treacle, lard, and milk in a saucepan and warm gently until the treacle and lard are melted.
5. Make a well in the dry ingredients, pour in the contents of the saucepan, and mix with a wooden spoon as if mixing a batter.
6. Beat well.
7. Pour into the tin.
8. Holding the tin level carry it carefully to the oven, and bake just above the centre for $1\frac{1}{4}$–$1\frac{1}{2}$ hours until firm in the centre.
9. Allow to cool a little, then loosen the edges with a knife, and turn carefully on to a cooling-tray.
10. Strip off the paper and turn right side up.

Note.

With parkin or gingerbread care must be taken when baking not to let a draught into the oven during the rising; this would cause it to sink in the middle.

GINGERBREAD MEN

4 oz. flour.	2 oz. sugar.
1 oz. margarine.	¼ teasp. bicarbonate of soda.
2 oz. syrup.	¼ teasp. ginger.

½ a beaten egg.

To make.

1. Prepare a very moderate oven.   Grease a baking-tray.
2. Sieve together the flour, bicarbonate of soda, and ginger. Add the sugar and mix.
3. Without making hot, melt the margarine and syrup and pour into a well in the centre of the flour, etc.
4. Mix, adding enough beaten egg to mix to a stiff dough.
5. Roll out ½ inch thick on a lightly floured board, and cut out with a gingerbread-man cutter or else divide the mixture into two pieces, and make two little men as follows:
     Divide each piece of mixture into six, then use one piece for the hat, one for the head, one to make two arms, one to make two legs, and two pieces for the body. Place together on a greased tin, sticking together with beaten egg.
6. Put currants for eyes, nose, mouth, and buttons.
7. Bake carefully 20–25 minutes until ginger in colour.
8. Allow to cool slightly, then lift carefully on to a cooling-tray, using a fish-slice to prevent breaking.

TREACLE TOFFEE

1 lb. Demerara sugar.
2 oz. margarine.
8 oz. black treacle or 4 oz. black treacle
and 4 oz. golden syrup.
A pinch of cream of tartar.
¼ pt. water.

To make.

1. Grease a Yorkshire-pudding tin.
2. Place the sugar and water together in a strong pan.   Stir with a tablespoon over a very gentle heat until the sugar has dissolved.   Do not allow this to boil.
3. Add the margarine, treacle, and cream of tartar, stir a little.
4. Bring to the boil, and boil gently without stirring until a hard ball is formed if a little is dropped into cold water.

5. Pour into the tin.

6. When firm enough, mark in squares with a knife and knock out of the tin when cold.

7. Store in a tin or jar with a lid—the toffee goes sticky if exposed to the air.

Happy Christmas!

CHRISTMAS DINNER

Roast pork or duck.
Apple sauce.
Sage and onion stuffing.
Boiled sprouts.
Roast potatoes or chip potatoes.
Gravy.

Roast chicken or turkey.
Sausages.
Bread sauce.
Forcemeat stuffing and balls.
Boiled sprouts.
Roast potatoes or chip potatoes.
Gravy.

Christmas pudding.
Sweet white sauce.
Mince-pies.　Cheese.
Cider cup, and orange squash for the children.

Roast Pork. Allow 30 minutes per lb. and 30 minutes extra. Cook the meat in a hot oven for the first 30 minutes, then reduce the heat to moderate, and baste frequently until the meat is thoroughly cooked. Dish the meat and make the gravy.

Roast Duck. Prepare the bird. Stuff at the tail end. Truss. Roast in a hot oven at first, then reduce to moderate and cook $1\frac{1}{2}$–2 hours, basting well. Test in the leg joints with a skewer, and when tender dish the bird and make the gravy.

Roast Chicken. Prepare the bird. Stuff at the head end. Truss. Cover the breast with fat bacon. Roast in a hot oven, basting well. Reduce the heat if necessary during cooking, and cover with a greased greaseproof paper to prevent the breast from becoming too brown. Time—1–$1\frac{1}{2}$ hours. Test the leg joints with a skewer, and when tender dish the bird and make the gravy.

Roast Turkey. Prepare the bird. Stuff at the head end. Truss. Cover the breast with fat bacon, and cook in a moderately hot oven, basting frequently. When the breast is sufficiently brown cover with greased greaseproof paper. Time—15 minutes per lb. weight after dressing. Test in the leg joint with skewer, and dish when cooked, then make the gravy.

Note.

1. If using an electric cooker basting is not required.
2. See *Look and Cook* for:
   Method of roasting.
   Making gravy.
   Making chip potatoes and roast potatoes.
   Cooking sprouts.
   Recipe for Christmas pudding and sweet white sauce, and rough puff or flaky pastry for the mince-pies.
3. The giblets from the birds, i.e. liver with gall bladder removed, heart, kidneys, and cleaned gizzard, together with the neck, should be washed, then simmered in order to make stock. This stock should be used for gravy.
4. When all the flesh has been carved from the bird the carcass should be broken in pieces, covered with water, and boiled gently several hours to make stock for soup.

SAGE AND ONION STUFFING

2 onions.	1 teasp. dried sifted sage
1½ oz. breadcrumbs.	(or 2 teasp. chopped fresh sage).
1 oz. margarine.	Seasoning.
	Beaten egg to bind.

To make.

1. Boil the onions, drain, chop finely.
2. Add breadcrumbs, seasoning, sage, and margarine. Mix together with a fork.
3. Add sufficient beaten egg to bind.
4. Use as stuffing, or reheat and serve separately.

YORKSHIRE SAVOURY PUDDING

(May be served with pork instead of sage and onion stuffing)

½ lb. onions.	1 dessertsp. dried sage or mixed herbs.
1 egg.	3 oz. suet.
8 oz. stale bread.	2 tablesp. oatmeal or 3 tablesp. rolled oats.

Salt and pepper to taste.

To make.

1. Soak bread in a little cold water for about 1 hour.
2. Chop the suet.   Peel and chop the raw onions.
3. Drain the bread, but do not squeeze dry.
4. Mix all the ingredients together using a fork.
5. Stir in the well-beaten egg.
6. Grease a Yorkshire-pudding tin 8 inches square, and pack the mixture into it.
7. Place in a fairly hot oven at first, and gradually reduce the heat to moderate, cooking for about 1 hour altogether.
8. When cooked and brown serve with roast pork, potatoes, greens, and gravy and apple sauce.

VEAL FORCEMEAT FOR A 10-LB. TURKEY

9 oz. breadcrumbs.	1 teasp. dried sifted thyme,
3 oz. suet.	or ½ tablesp. fresh thyme.
2 tablesp. chopped parsley.	Grated rind of ½ lemon.
Seasoning.	A little chopped bacon if available.

Beaten egg to bind.

To make.

1. Prepare and mix together all the ingredients and add enough beaten egg to make the mixture hold together if pressed in the hand.   Use a fork to mix.
2. Stuff the turkey at the neck end, avoiding packing too tightly, as the breadcrumbs swell on cooking.
3. Shape extra stuffing into small balls, coat with egg and crumbs, and fry; this may be done on Boxing Day to give a renewed supply of stuffing.

APPLE SAUCE
(See p. 64.)

BREAD SAUCE

1 pt. milk.	4 oz. breadcrumbs.
1 large onion.	Pepper and salt.
1 clove.	1 oz. margarine.

Cream from the top of the milk.

To make.

1. Peel the onion and stick a clove into it.   Lightly grease a saucepan, and simmer in it the onion in the milk.
2. When tender squeeze the onion with a spoon against the side of the pan, and lift it out.
3. Sift in the breadcrumbs.
4. Add the margarine and stir over gentle heat until boiling. Add pepper and salt and taste.
5. Stir in a little cream if available.   The sauce should be a thick creamy consistency.

MINCEMEAT
(makes 6 lb.)

1½ lb. apples.	¼ lb. mixed peel.
1 lb. brown sugar.	¼ nutmeg.
1 lb. currants.	½ teasp. mixed spice.
½ lb. Valencia raisins.	½ teasp. ground ginger.
¼ lb. sultanas.	Rind and juice of 2 lemons.

¾ lb. suet.

To make.

1. Wash and pick over the dried fruit—rub in an old clean tea-towel, then spread on a meat dish and leave to dry over-night at ordinary kitchen temperature.
2. Have ready six clean, dry, 1-lb. jam jars.
3. Peel, core, and chop the apples, and put into a large mixing-bowl.
4. Add the sugar, spices, chopped suet, chopped currants, and

E

raisins, together with the grated rind and squeezed juice of the lemons.

5. Mix with a wooden spoon until juicy.
6. Pack gently into the jars.
7. Cover with greaseproof paper and tie down. Store in a cool, dry place.
8. Stir before using as the juice settles to the bottom.

DECORATED CHRISTMAS CAKE

5 oz. margarine.
5 oz. castor sugar.
3 eggs.
6 oz. plain flour.
½ teasp. baking-powder.
1 lb. fruit—currants, raisins, sultanas.
2 oz. each—almonds, glacé cherries, mixed peel.
½ teasp. spice if liked.
1 dessertsp. black treacle if liked—this darkens the cake.

To make.

1. Wash the dried fruit well and pick it over. Rub in a clean, old tea-towel, spread on a meat dish, cover, and leave in the ordinary kitchen temperature to dry overnight.
2. Put the almonds into a small saucepan, cover with cold water, bring to the boil. Strain off the water, then rub the almonds between the thumb and first finger to remove the skins; this is called 'blanching.' Chop the almonds. Chop the peel. Cut the cherries in four.
3. Grease a 7-inch or 8-inch cake-tin, and line with double greased greaseproof paper. (See *Look and Cook*, p. 117.) Then wrap and tie the outside of the tin with brown paper to give added protection during the long cooking. Prepare a fairly hot oven.
4. Sieve together the flour, baking-powder, and spice.
5. Cream the margarine and sugar until light and creamy;

this must be done very thoroughly. Do not on any account melt the margarine; if it is very hard the mixing-bowl may be held for a minute or two in a washing-up bowl of hot water to soften the margarine slightly, but if the margarine is allowed to become oily it gives the cake a coarse texture.

6. Break the eggs separately, beat and add little by little. Take care not to add too much at once, and so cause the mixture to curdle.

7. If signs of curdling occur, i.e. if the egg does not beat in completely, stir in a spoonful of the flour.

8. When all the egg is added, stir in all the fruit, and then the flour, adding very little milk if required to mix to a dropping consistency. Stir in the black treacle if used.

9. Pack carefully into the tin, hollow out a hole in the centre about 3 inches across and 1 inch deep, then make the edges perfectly flat. This helps to make a level top for icing.

10. Bake just above the centre of the oven. After 10 minutes, without opening the oven door, reduce the heat to moderate and bake 2½–3 hours in all. Cover with greased greaseproof paper if necessary towards the end of cooking.

11. Test with a skewer, which may be sticky with fruit, but should not be sticky with mixture.

12. Cool slightly, then lift the cake carefully from the tin on to a cooling-tray. If the tin has a loose bottom the tin may be removed as follows:

Invert a 1-pint basin on the table. Carefully place the cake-tin upon it. Gently lower the sides of the tin down to the table. Lift the cake on the bottom of the tin to a cooling-tray.

Remove the bottom carefully, leaving the paper on the cake until it is decorated.

OVEN HEATS

Electric

Set at 450° F.

Switch to 350° F. on putting the cake into the oven.

After 1 hour switch to 300° F.

Reduce further if necessary.

Gas

Set at Regulo 6.

Put in the cake, and after 10 minutes turn to Regulo 3.

Bake at Regulo 3, lowering after 2 hours if necessary.

A MORE ECONOMICAL CHRISTMAS CAKE RECIPE

4 oz. castor sugar.
4 oz. margarine.
2 eggs.
6 oz. self-raising flour.
Pinch of salt.

12 oz. mixed fruit.
3 drops almond essence.
3 drops vanilla essence.
1 dessertsp. black treacle.
A little milk.

Make and bake as above—this cake will take about $2\frac{1}{4}$ hours to bake.

ALMOND PASTE

This quantity will be sufficient for the top of either of the foregoing cakes.

4 oz. castor sugar. $\frac{1}{2}$ lb. ground almonds.
4 oz. icing sugar.   Beaten egg.
3 drops almond essence.

To make.

1. Roll and sieve the icing sugar.
2. Mix together the icing and castor sugar and the ground almonds.
3. Beat the egg. Pour half this into a well in the centre of the almonds. Add the almond essence to this.
4. Mix with a wooden spoon, adding more beaten egg if required to mix to a stiff though not crumbly consistency.
5. Work until smooth in texture, then use.

MOCK ALMOND PASTE

4 oz. margarine.   ¼ pt. water.
6 oz. sugar.   ½ teasp. almond essence.
10 oz. soya flour.

To make.

1. Put the margarine, sugar, and water into a saucepan. Stir over gentle heat until the margarine has melted, then bring to the boil.
2. Remove from the heat. Add the almond essence, and gradually mix in the soya flour.
3. Taste. Add a little more essence if required, then knead until quite smooth.

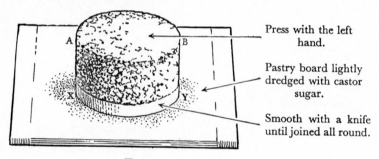

Press with the left hand.

Pastry board lightly dredged with castor sugar.

Smooth with a knife until joined all round.

TO APPLY ALMOND PASTE

To apply the almond paste.

1. Dredge a pastry board with castor sugar.
2. Cut off a piece of almond paste about 1½ inches square. Wrap this to use for the making of holly, mistletoe, and crackers as on the photographed cake (frontispiece).
3. Shape the rest into a round and roll out to the exact size of the top of the cake.
4. Remove the papers from the cake and brush the top of the cake with beaten egg or with very little melted apricot jam.

5. Make sure the almond 'round' is loose on the board, then stand the cake with the brushed top to the almond.

6. Place the left hand firmly on the cake and press, then with a pastry knife in the right hand smooth the almond paste until it joins the cake all round, and the sides of the cake and the almond are in a straight line. (See diagram, p. 123.)

7. Bend down so that you can see if the icing is level. AB should be parallel to XY.

8. Carefully lift the cake on to an inverted plate.

9. Cover lightly and leave the almond paste to dry for at least 24 hours, or lift the cake into the storage tin and leave the lid half off.

Note.

If the top of the cake is not level a small rim of almond paste should be built up first. This must be done on to a surface brushed with egg. The rest of the almond should then be rolled and applied as described above.

ROYAL ICING

This quantity is sufficient to decorate the foregoing Christmas cake (see photograph, frontispiece).

1 white of egg.	½ teasp. lemon juice.
6–8 oz. icing sugar.	A touch of blue colouring.

To make.

1. Separate the yolk from the white of the egg, taking care not to get the least trace of yolk on the white.

2. Put the white in a mixing-bowl.

3. Roll and sieve the icing sugar.

4. Add ⅓ of the sugar and mix in and beat with a wooden spoon. Beat well, but do not whip up as this causes a bubbly icing. Beat for 5 minutes.

5. Add the second ⅓ of sugar and continue to beat well. At this stage add the lemon juice, and just a touch of blue-colouring from a skewer. This whitens the icing, but care must be taken not to add too much blue.

6. Gradually add enough of the remaining sugar until the icing is sufficiently stiff to draw up in points on the surface. This is then ready to use to produce the effect of snow on the cake.

Note.

Royal icing, when mixed, must be used at once or covered with a clean damp towel to prevent drying.

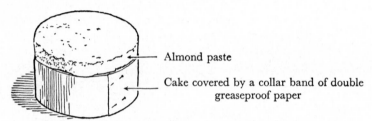

— Almond paste

— Cake covered by a collar band of double greaseproof paper

To APPLY ROYAL ICING

To apply the royal icing.

1. First to ensure that the royal icing makes a level edge, as in the photographed cake (frontispiece), a collar band of greaseproof paper must be pinned round, so that when the icing is applied it is even round the sides. (See diagram.)

   Note that the double collar band of greaseproof paper is measured and pinned round from the lowest point of almond paste, e.g. if most of the almond paste is $2\frac{1}{4}$ inches from the bottom of the cake, but in one place it is $2\frac{1}{8}$ inches from the bottom, then cut the double greaseproof paper exactly $2\frac{1}{8}$ inches wide, and long enough to go round the cake. Measure round the cake with a piece of string, and make the collar $1\frac{1}{2}$ inches longer to allow for pinning. Remember two pins in and two pins out when the icing is dry!

2. Using a spotlessly clean palette knife or pastry knife, spread the royal icing over the almond paste, bringing it over the sides until it just comes over the collar.

3. Spread quickly and evenly, then with a light flick of the wrist draw the icing up in points to look like snow. If you intend to have a central decoration leave a flat piece here, but if you intend to model a snow scene with a house and little trees leave a flat bit where these will go and smooth a pathway to the house.

4. Leave to dry.

5. After about $\frac{1}{2}$ hour very carefully remove the pins and put back in the box. Then, using a knife to help if necessary, carefully peel off the paper collar, making the edge neat with the blade of the knife.

6. Leave to become quite dry.

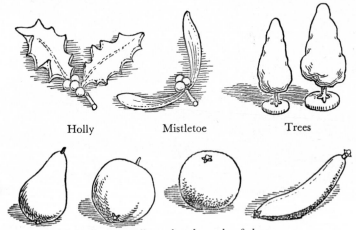

Holly   Mistletoe   Trees

Fruits: stalks and ends made of cloves

DECORATIONS FOR THE CAKE

To make the models.

It is much more fun to make your own decorations than to buy them. The models are done in much the same way as models are made in glitter-wax or plasticine. If making leaves or flowers try to have one to copy, e.g. holly, mistletoe, violets.

Roll the almond paste on a pastry board lightly dredged with castor sugar.

Cut the leaf to the shape and size, using a vegetable knife or potato-peeler, or a thimble might help to shape the holly leaves.

Nip out the points carefully with your fingers, then mark in the veins to make them look real.

Put to dry over bits of crumpled paper on a plate, so that the leaves dry slightly curled and not flat like pennies.   Then make berries of the correct size to go with the leaves.

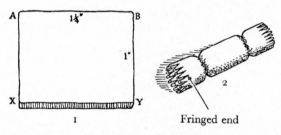

TO MAKE THE CRACKER

For the crackers: Cut out oblongs of almond paste after rolling it thinly (see Diagram 1).   Roll AB to XY, so making a neat sausage shape.   Hold this against the board, and carefully with a skewer make slight dints round the cracker a third of the way down from each end (see Diagram 2).   Then fringe the ends slightly with a skewer.

When the models are dry they should be painted with icing colourings, which may be bought from a health food stores, grocer's shop, or chemist's.   Yellow, blue, and red are useful colours, as most colours can be mixed from these.

Yellow plus blue=Green.   For mistletoe green add more yellow to make a yellow-green.   For holly green add more blue to make a blue-green.

*F

Yellow plus ⎫
blue plus red ⎬ = Brown.   A little spot of brown in the end
             makes the berries more real—the holly
             berries are first painted red—a little yellow
             may be needed in the red.   Mistletoe
             berries are the colour of the almond paste.

The crackers are gay if painted bright red and all alike.

Small trees to put round a model house may be made from cone-shaped pieces of almond paste stuck on to a clove; then the clove should be placed on a small almond paste base.

Almond paste fruits are attractive, and cloves make stalks for apples and pears and ends for oranges.

When dry paint them to resemble the real fruits.

Stand the bottles of colour on a plate.   Use economically and never dip the paint brushes into the bottles or the colours will become mixed.   Rinse the paint brush in a basin of cold water and dry on a rag when using different colours.

To stick decorations to the icing.

Use a little freshly made royal icing applied invisibly under each decoration.   Place carefully where you wish them to stay.

To make the decorations glitter.

Sprinkle with frost.

To make frost.

Buy 2 oz. gum arabic crystals from the chemist.

1. Place 1 tablespoonful of the gum in a small saucepan.
2. Add 2 tablespoonfuls of water.
3. Stir over very gentle heat to melt.
* 4. Strain through muslin.
5. Paint this gum with a clean pastry brush on to several dinner plates.
6. Place to dry in a very moderate oven.
7. When quite dry brush off the dried glaze from the plates.

Use a piece of tissue-paper and brush on to a sheet of greaseproof paper. Repeat until used. The tiny specks will glitter—this is edible frost, and may be sprinkled on the models or on sweets.

8. Store in a screw-topped jar.

* *Note.*

This strained gum may be painted on dried models. This makes them glossy and helps them to keep.

To finish the cake.

Pin a collar of cellophane paper round the cake exactly the width of the cake below the icing. Tie this round with a narrow red ribbon. After making a pretty bow remove the pin.

A silver board is useful to stand the cake on instead of a dish. After Christmas this should be rubbed over, wrapped up, and used on subsequent occasions.

BIRTHDAY CAKES

1. Apply the almond paste as for Christmas cake.
2. When dry prepare the cake for icing by pinning round a tight collar band of greaseproof paper as described on p. 125.
3. Make the royal icing as on p. 124, but, after adding the second ½ of icing sugar, the lemon juice, and a touch of blue colouring, add only a little more icing sugar so that the icing is sufficiently stiff to support the wooden spoon if you stand it in the middle, but not stiff enough to stay in points as for the snow icing.
4. Spread this evenly over the cake and down the sides just on to the collar band. Make the surface even by smoothing with a palette knife dipped and shaken out of a jug of boiling water. Work quickly. Do not make the icing wet.

5. Leave to dry in ordinary warmth.

6. When firm but not quite set remove the pins, and with the help of a knife remove the collar band.

7. Leave to become quite dry.

To pipe the cake.

1. Draw a pattern on greaseproof paper exactly the size of the top of the cake.   (Draw round the cake-tin to obtain this.)

2. Plan your design on this.

3. When the cake is firm and dry, and not before, place the pattern on the cake, and with a clean hat-pin prick the design lightly on the icing.

4. Prepare royal icing of exactly the same consistency as that for the snow (see p. 124).

5. Make several paper piping bags (see below).

6. Practise piping on a plate and scrape off, keeping the rest of the icing covered with a damp cloth all the time.   A plain writing pipe and an eight-pointed star are two good tubes to possess—pretty decorations can be made with these.

7. Pipe the design.

8. Decorate the cake with coloured flowers modelled in almond paste ; or a few crystallized flowers, applied artistically with leaves and stems modelled in almond paste, make an attractive decoration.   Silver balls sometimes give a pretty effect.

TO MAKE, FILL, AND USE A PIPING BAG

1. Cut a 9-inch square of greaseproof paper.

2. Fold across the diagonal.   Crease firmly.

3. Cut—then place together to make a double bag.

4. Holding the centre of XY at B with the thumb and finger

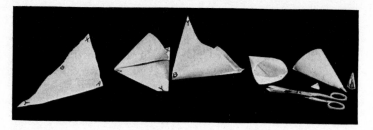

To make a Piping Bag

of the left hand, with the right hand fold X to A, then take Y round to A, enclosing A.

5. Hold points XAY together, and shuffle to make a sharp point at B.
6. Crease the corners down twice backwards to make a firm edge, and hold the bag tightly together.
7. Cut off ½ inch at the bottom B.
8. Insert the piping tube (see photograph).
9. Fill the bag half full of royal icing of a piping consistency.
10. Fold down the top to press the icing together and make a ledge on which to rest the thumb of the right hand.

Note.

Always have several bags in readiness.

FRUIT PUNCH

1 level tablesp. marmalade.	½ pt. water.
1 level dessertsp. syrup.	2 tablesp. orange squash.
¼–½ level teasp. ground ginger.	1 tablesp. lemon squash.
1 pt. fresh tea.	

To make.

1. Mix everything together.
2. Strain.
3. Serve very cold.

Local Dishes

Here are three examples of local dishes: East Riding Curd Tart, West Country Lardy Cake, and Scotch Shortbread. You will find other recipes in *Look and Cook* and in other parts of this book, e.g. Cornish Pasties, Yorkshire Pudding, Tea Cakes and Parkin, Lancashire Hot-Pot and Eccles Cakes, Shrewsbury Cakes and Chelsea Buns.

CURD TART

4 oz. short pastry.

Filling

2 oz. margarine.	2 oz. currants.
2 oz. castor sugar.	Grated rind of ½ lemon.
1 egg.	¼ lb. curds (see below).

To make.

1. Make 4 oz. good short pastry and line a flan-ring (see p. 60).
2. Cream the margarine and sugar, and when light and fluffy add the well-beaten egg gradually, beating well in.
3. Wash the currants, and stir these in together with the grated lemon rind and the curds.
4. Spread the mixture in the pastry case.
5. Bake in a fairly hot oven for 15 minutes, then reduce the heat a little so that the pastry cooks thoroughly and the mixture sets and turns a rich golden colour. Time: 30–35 minutes altogether.
6. Carefully remove the flan-ring.
7. Lift with a fish-slice to a cooling-tray.
8. Serve when cold.

CURDS

These may sometimes be bought in the market or can be made as follows:

1. Measure 1 pint of milk.
2. Blend 1 level dessertspoonful flour with a little of the milk and add 1 teaspoonful vinegar to this.

3. Boil up the rest of the milk, and pour when boiling on to the blended flour and the vinegar.   Stir well all the time.
4. Return to the pan, stir until boiling, and let the curds boil up.
5. Cool in a basin.
6. Strain through muslin.
7. When the curd is dry break it with a fork and use it in the mixture.

Note.

1. Curds may also be made using fresh milk and rennet, and following the directions on the bottle of rennet.
2. Raw milk which has soured produces a curd which may be filtered and used.

LARDY CAKE

½ lb. white dough.	3 oz. mixed dried fruit.
3 oz. lard.	½ oz. peel.
3 oz. granulated sugar.	

To make.

1. Take ½ lb. of risen dough (see *Look and Cook*, p. 137).
2. Grease and warm an 8-inch square tin.
3. Flour a board and shape and roll the dough into an oblong.
4. Divide the fat, fruit, and sugar into two piles.
5. Put half the fat in pats on the top two-thirds of the strip of dough (as for flaky pastry).   Sprinkle on one pile of fruit and sugar.   Press lightly with the hand.
6. Fold the bottom edge of the dough to the middle and then the top down.   Seal the edges.   Quarter turn.
7. Re-roll.
8. Repeat 5 and 6.
9. Roll into a square to fit the tin.
10. Press well into the tin.
11. Score across the top diagonally in both directions to make a trellis effect.
12. Cover and prove for 20 minutes.
13. Bake in a fairly hot oven 40–45 minutes until a good golden colour and cooked through.
14. Loosen carefully and turn out on to a cooling-tray.

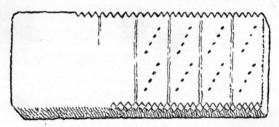

SHORTBREAD

Roll into strip.   Mark and prick decoratively.   Mark
carefully into fingers 1 in. wide.

SHORTBREAD

6 oz. plain flour.   4 oz. butter or margarine.
2 oz. castor sugar.

To make.

1. Sieve the flour into a bowl. Add the sugar, and the margarine in one piece.
2. Knead the flour and sugar into the margarine.
3. When firm and no longer crumbly lift on to a lightly floured board. Knead into an oblong shape.
4. Roll into an oblong about 3 inches wide and $\frac{1}{2}$ inch thick.
5. Smooth down the edges with a knife, making them quite straight.
6. Decorate the long straight sides with a potato-peeler (see diagram).
7. Mark the shortbread into fingers about 1 inch wide.
8. Prick decoratively. Sprinkle with castor sugar.
9. Lift carefully on to a flat greased tin—a baking-tray used upside-down is the easiest to use, as there is no ridge.
10. Bake carefully in a very moderate oven until golden brown —about 30 minutes.
11. Allow to cool slightly.
12. Cut carefully through the markings and lift to a cooling-tray (photograph, p. 14).

4

PRESERVING FRUIT AND VEGETABLES

Preserves

Everyone who is able to do so should make some preserves each year.

REASONS FOR PRESERVING

1. Preserved fruit and vegetables ensure a supply of protective foods in winter months when fresh supplies are expensive and scarce.

2. Surplus fruit and vegetables are preserved for winter use and so prevent waste in the summer when there is too much to use all at once.

3. Preserves add variety, colour, and flavour to the meals.

4. Pickles and chutneys make otherwise flavourless dishes appetizing.

5. Bottled and canned fruits and vegetables are easy to use and make good emergency meals.

6. Home-made jams, jellies, and marmalades are often better in flavour than commercial ones.

7. It is often cheaper to make preserves than to buy them, especially in country districts.

THE MEANING OF PRESERVATION

Nature intends all plants to begin as seed, to grow, flower, form fruit, and seed, and finally to decay so that the seed is scattered to make new young plants.

When fruit and vegetables are preserved the aim is to prevent decay, and to preserve them in the form in which they are usually eaten.

THE ORGANISMS THAT CAUSE DECAY

Yeasts. These are tiny plants present in the air, which settle on ripe fruit and cause it to ferment, and to have a winy smell and taste.

Moulds. These are also present in the air; they settle on the damp surface of fruit and vegetables, and grow very quickly. The moulds penetrate the skins and cause the fruit to soften.

Bacteria. These are also tiny organisms that cause the fruit and vegetables to become rotten and to break up, thus exposing the seed.

In order to preserve the fruit and vegetables at the correct stage it is necessary either to kill the yeasts, moulds, and bacteria present and to prevent the fruit and vegetables from coming into further contact with them, or to add substances which will prevent their growth.

	Methods of Preserving Fruit and Vegetables	Methods of Destroying or Preventing the Growth of Yeasts, Moulds, and Bacteria
1.	Drying	Complete absence of moisture
2.	Salting	Strong salt conditions
3.	Freezing	Very cold conditions
4.	Jamming	Very sweet conditions
5.	Pickling	Acid conditions due to the vinegar
6.	Bottling and canning	Prolonged heat kills the organisms, and air-tight containers prevent further contact

SIMPLE METHODS OF PRESERVING

Some methods of preserving, such as freezing or canning, need expensive equipment, but most homes have pans, spoons, and bowls that are suitable for the other methods of preserving.

GENERAL RULES

1. Do not attempt too big quantities for the equipment available.
2. Preserve the foods that will be most useful.
3. Preserve when the fruit is in season; it is cheapest to buy and at its best for eating.
4. Take good care of preserving equipment when it is not in use. Bottling jars should be stored carefully after using the preserves so that the parts are complete and in good order for the next preserving season.
5. Follow recipes and instructions accurately for successful preserving.

Jam-making

Jam should have a bright colour, a fruity flavour, and a well-set, but not too stiff, consistency. A good jam will keep well.

Jam is a combination of fruit and sugar. The fruit contains

pectin and acid. Pectin is a substance which, with the acid, helps to make the jam set and give it a good colour and flavour.

EQUIPMENT FOR MAKING JAM

1. A strong preserving-pan or large saucepan.
2. A large wooden spoon.
3. A large mixing-bowl, colander, plate, small jug.
4. Jam jars, jam covers, waxed circles, rubber bands, and labels.

EQUIPMENT FOR MAKING JAM

GENERAL METHOD FOR MAKING ALL JAMS

1. Read the recipe carefully, check the amount of sugar and fruit required. Buy a packet of jam covers: these generally include waxed circles, rubber bands, and labels. Estimate the number of jars required. Wash the jars very thoroughly, removing old labels. Rinse in cold water and dry with a non-fluffy tea-towel.

2. To estimate the approximate number of jars required, multiply the amount of sugar in the recipe by $\frac{100}{60}$; this allows 60 per cent sugar content. The result gives the number of pounds of jam, e.g. 6 lb. sugar $\times \frac{100}{60}$ gives 10 lb. jam, therefore 10 jars will be required.

3. Prepare the fruit according to kind. Top and tail gooseberries, remove green hulls and leaves from raspberries and strawberries, take out stalks from plums, and use a fork to strip off the currants from their stems.

4. Pick out any mouldy or bruised fruit. Bad parts can often be cut out of larger fruits. Weigh the fruit, wash carefully in a large bowl of cold water, drain in a colander. Raspberries are not usually washed but should be very clean.

5. Lightly grease the preserving-pan with a butter paper. Put the fruit in the preserving-pan, add the amount of water stated in the recipe, bring slowly to the boil, then reduce the heat and simmer gently. Stir occasionally. Keep the wooden spoon on a plate. This first cooking of the fruit without the sugar breaks up the fruit and draws out the pectin and the acid.

6. Continue cooking the fruit until it is broken up and thick and pulpy. The time of cooking varies with the fruit.

7. Weigh the sugar. Put it into a dry bowl and stand it in a warm place.

8. Put the washed jam jars in a warm place to become hot and quite dry. A cool oven is useful for this, but the jars must be warmed slowly to prevent cracking.

9. When the fruit is a thick pulp draw it off the heat. Add the sugar, replace over the heat and stir until the sugar has dissolved, and then allow the jam to boil quickly. The jam must not boil until the sugar has dissolved. Boiling quickly gives a better flavour and colour, but it must not be allowed to splash too much.

10. After 10 minutes test for setting point.   This can be done in several ways:

    (1) Use a sugar thermometer or one which registers to 300 or more degrees Fahrenheit.   Boil the jam until the thermometer reads 220° F.   Stand the thermometer in a jug of hot water before and after testing the jam.   Do not allow the bulb of the thermometer to rest on the bottom of the pan.

    (2) *Wrinkle test.*   Put a little jam on a clean saucer, stand it in a cool place for a few minutes.   Push the jam gently, and if ready it will wrinkle on the surface. It is better to remove the jam from the heat whilst testing in this way.

    (3) *Flake test.*   Dip the wooden spoon in the jam, hold up above a plate, and twist the spoon round to cool the jam a little.   Hold the spoon sideways above the plate; most of the jam will run straight off, but if the jam is ready the last few drops will cling together, and form pointed flakes before falling.

       The flake test is very reliable, and is preferred by most people.

11. When the jam sets remove from the heat.   Marmalade, strawberry jam, and any other jam with large pieces of fruit should be allowed to cool in the pan for several minutes; this helps to distribute the shreds of marmalade or the fruit evenly through each jar.   Other jam is poured into the jars at once.

12. It is better to close outside doors and avoid sudden draughts which might crack the hot jars.   Stand the hot, dry jars on a pastry board or wooden table.   Lift the preserving-pan carefully on to a firm pan-stand near to the jars. Have ready a jug and a plate.

13. Use a tablespoon and remove any scum from the surface of the jam.   It is wasteful to skim off too much, and most of the small air bubbles will disappear.

14. Dip the jug into the jam, hold the plate underneath to catch the drips, and fill the hot jars until the jam is level with the top; this is important as the jam shrinks on cooling. When the jam becomes too low to fill the jug stand it on the plate and pour the jam into it from the preserving-pan. Scrape out the pan, the jug, and the plate to fill the last jar.

15. Fit the waxed circles, waxed side down, over the surface of the jam. The circle should lie flat. This is important as the waxed circle keeps out the air.

16. Use a clean cloth wrung out in hot water to clean the rim and sides of each jar.

17. The jam should be covered, or tied down, at once or when it is quite cold. Protect the jam with a clean muslin if it is to be covered when cold.

18. To cover jam follow the instructions on the packet of jam covers. Cellophane and parchment covers are moistened on the upper surface before covering. This makes them stretch so that they dry with a smooth tight surface. Rubber bands or soft white string are used to keep the covers in place.

19. When the jam is quite cold label with the kind of jam and the date. Keep the labels level on all the jars.

20. When the jam is quite ready store in a cool, dry, dark place. All jam is better used before the next season's jam is made.

Jam Recipes

RASPBERRY JAM

As raspberries break up almost at once no water need be added, and the cooking time is reduced.

6 lb. raspberries.   6 lb. sugar.

To make approximately 10 lb. jam.

To make.

Follow the general instructions for making jam with these special points:

1. Put the fruit in the pan and heat slowly until the juice begins to appear, then simmer until the fruit is broken down.
2. Boil with the sugar for only 5 minutes, and then test for setting point.

BLACKCURRANT JAM

Blackcurrants are rich in pectin and therefore need more sugar in proportion to fruit to make good jam. The skins of blackcurrants harden when the sugar is added, therefore the first cooking with the water, before adding the sugar, must be very thorough.

4 lb. blackcurrants.   6 lb. sugar.
3 pt. water.

To make approximately 10 lb. jam.

To make.

Follow the general instructions for making jam with the following special points:

1. The large amount of water allows the skins to soften and burst. Simmer the fruit and water together until all the currants have broken up and the water has been driven off to give a thick pulp. This takes at least 30 minutes.
2. Blackcurrant jam should set quite quickly once the sugar has dissolved. Test for setting point after boiling for 5 minutes.

PLUM JAM

Victoria plums and Golden plums make good jam. Greengages may also be used.

6 lb. plums.   6 lb. sugar.
1 pt. water.

To make approximately 10 lb. jam.

To make.

Follow the general instructions for making jam, but note the special points below:

1. A good flavour is obtained if a few of the stones from ripe plums are cracked, and the whole nut or kernel taken out and cooked with the jam.
2. Stones can be removed from some varieties of plums before beginning to cook. If the stones are difficult to remove when the fruit is cut in half it is better to cook them in the jam and to take out as many as possible as they rise to the surface. A small wire basket may be fixed to the inside edge of the preserving-pan to put the stones in; this allows any jam to drip back.

GOOSEBERRY JAM

Green gooseberries are used for jam. The colour of the jam varies with the ripeness and variety of the fruit. Boiling for a long time with the sugar gives a red gooseberry jam.

5 lb. gooseberries.   6 lb. sugar.
2 pt. water.

To make approximately 10 lb. jam.

To make.

Follow the general instructions for making jam.

Jelly

Jelly is a mixture of fruit and sugar as for jam, but the fruit is cooked to a pulp and then strained to give a clear liquid.

Only those fruits rich in pectin should be made into jelly, and it is very important to extract all the pectin from the fruit before straining.

FRUITS SUITABLE FOR JELLY

Cooking apples.   Crab apples.
Red currants.   Gooseberries.

Some fruits are mixed together to give jellies with a good flavour and set:

Blackberry and apple.
Redcurrant and raspberry.

GENERAL INSTRUCTIONS FOR MAKING JELLY

1. Follow the instructions for making jam with regard to preparation, testing, and finishing.

2. Wash the fruit, but do not remove the stalks.

3. Put the fruit and water into the preserving-pan and simmer slowly for about 1 hour or until the fruit is quite broken up.

4. For straining use a jelly stand or a stool or chair placed upside-down on a table. Tie a strong, fine, linen cloth or a felt jelly-bag so that it hangs down from the legs of the stool, and place a basin underneath. A cloth with tapes stitched across each corner makes a useful jelly-bag. Scald the cloth by pouring boiling water through before straining the jelly.

5. Empty the water from the basin. The basin should be large enough to take the juice but small enough to slip between the legs of the stool. Pour the cooked fruit carefully into the cloth and leave to drain until no drips come through the cloth. This takes a few hours and it is often left to drip overnight. The bag should not be squeezed or the jelly will be cloudy.

6. Measure the juice and weigh out 1 lb. sugar for each pint of juice. If the juice is very watery allow ¾ lb. sugar to each pint.

7. Prepare the clean, warm jars, as jelly sets quickly when it is ready. Small fancy jars or ½-lb. jars are used for jelly.

8. Pour the juice into the preserving-pan and bring to the boil, remove from the heat and add the sugar. Stir until it is dissolved and then boil quickly without stirring until setting point is reached. Use the flake test. A jelly rich in pectin will set after 10 minutes' boiling, but some fruits

require 15 to 20 minutes. A better colour and flavour is obtained if the jelly will set quickly, but this depends on the amount of pectin extracted in the first cooking.

9. Skim the jelly carefully, using a tablespoon.
10. Pour into jars as quickly as possible as jelly may begin to set in the pan.
11. Finish with waxed circles and cover and label as for jam.

Jelly Recipes

BLACKBERRY AND APPLE JELLY

4 lb. blackberries.	1 lb. sugar to each pint
2 lb. cooking apples.	of juice.
2 pt. water.	

To make.

1. Follow the general instructions for making jelly.
2. Wash the apples and cut up without peeling.
3. Put the apples and blackberries in the preserving-pan, add the water, and simmer until quite broken up.
4. Strain through a jelly cloth and leave to drip.
5. Measure the juice and weigh out 1 lb. sugar to each pint. Put the juice in the preserving-pan, bring to the boil. Remove from the heat to add the sugar. Stir until the sugar is dissolved.
6. Boil quickly without stirring, and after 10 minutes test for setting point.
7. When setting point is reached skim and finish as for jam.

MINT JELLY

A delicious jelly can be made from apples flavoured with mint. Apple jelly is made in the same way without the mint and the colouring.

3 lb. green cooking apples.	2 lemons.
2 pt. water.	A large bunch of fresh mint.
1 lb. sugar for each 1 pt. of juice.	A few drops of green colouring.

To make.

1. Follow the general instructions for making jelly.
2. Wash the apples and cut up without peeling.
3. Put the apples, water, lemon juice, and some of the washed mint in a preserving-pan, simmer until the apples have formed a thick pulp.
4. Strain through a scalded jelly cloth and leave to drip.
5. When ready tie up a bunch of washed mint. Bruise the leaves with a rolling-pin or wooden spoon.
6. Measure the juice, weigh the sugar, bring the juice to the boil. Add the sugar and stir until dissolved.
7. Remove the pan from the heat and suspend the bunch of mint in the jelly. The string may be tied to the handle.
8. Bring the jelly to the boil, and boil quickly without stirring until setting point is reached. Test after boiling for 10 minutes.
9. When ready skim carefully. Add a few drops of green colouring and stir until evenly mixed. The jelly should be a pale green, and should taste and smell of mint.
10. Pour into the warm, dry jars and finish as for jam.

Note.

Crab apples make a delicious pinky gold apple jelly. They should be just under-ripe for the best jelly, as ripe fruit contains less pectin and makes a cloudy jelly.

Marmalade

Marmalade is made from bitter oranges or a mixture of bitter oranges with other citrus fruits, such as grape-fruit, sweet oranges, or lemons. The best bitter oranges are Seville oranges. Bitter oranges are in season during January and February.

Some marmalade is thick with chunky pieces of peel, and some is clear with very fine shreds of peel.

SPECIAL POINTS IN MAKING MARMALADE

1. The pectin is contained in the white pith and the pips.
2. To extract enough pectin to make the marmalade set the peel and pips are soaked in cold water, and then cooked very thoroughly before adding the sugar.
3. Marmalade usually needs added acid to help it to set. This is often added in the form of lemon juice.
4. Marmalade will lose its colour, flavour, and power of setting if boiled much longer than 15 to 20 minutes with the sugar; therefore the first cooking without the sugar must be very thorough.
5. After skimming allow the marmalade to set a little in the preserving-pan so that the shreds of peel will be evenly distributed through each jar.

THICK SEVILLE ORANGE MARMALADE

(To make approximately 10 lb. marmalade)

2 lb. Seville oranges.	6 pt. water.
2 sweet oranges.	6 lb. sugar.
Juice of 2 lemons.	

To make.

1. Read the general instructions for making jam.
2. Wash the fruit very thoroughly in cold water.
3. Cut the fruit in half. Squeeze out the juice and pips. Tie the pips in a piece of muslin.
4. Put the juice from the oranges with the lemon juice and bag of pips in a large bowl.
5. Slice up the skins and as much of the pulp of the fruit as possible. Add to the juice and pips.
6. Add sufficient of the 6 pints of water to cover. Leave to stand overnight. Make a note of the amount of water still to be added. Cover the bowl with a cloth.
7. Put the fruit and the rest of the water into the preserving-pan, and simmer gently for 2 hours. When ready the

peel should be soft enough to crush easily between thumb and finger, and the water will be reduced.

8. Prepare the clean warm jars as for making jam. Add the sugar, stir until dissolved, then boil quickly until setting point is reached. Test after 10 minutes.

9. Skim, then cool a little in the pan. Finish as for jam. Marmalade is covered with waxed circles when hot, but is usually tied down when quite cold.

Bottling

Bottled fruit is a means of preserving fruit by sterilizing it in bottles, and then making the bottles air-tight.

Bottled fruit makes a welcome change in the winter.

There are two methods used for bottling:

1. The Water-bath method.
2. The Oven method.

The water-bath method is the more accurate and is safer and is suitable for bottling all fruits. The oven method can be used for soft fruits, and is particularly useful for bottling small quantities of fruit.

EQUIPMENT NEEDED FOR BOTTLING

1. Preserving-jars, rubber bands, lids, screw bands, or clips. There are many types of bottling tops which can be bought to use on sound jam jars. These are useful for very small quantities, but if much fruit is to be preserved it is better to buy a few preserving-jars. These may be used from year to year, and only the rubber bands and occasionally the lids need to be replaced.

There are two main types of preserving-jar:

(1) The screw band type.
(2) The clip type.

All types have a rubber band and a lid.

EQUIPMENT FOR BOTTLING FRUIT

2. A large bowl and a colander for washing the fruit.
3. A saucepan to make the syrup.
4. A jug.
5. A fine strainer or a piece of butter-muslin through which to strain the syrup if necessary.

GENERAL INSTRUCTIONS FOR BOTTLING FRUIT

(1) *The Syrup.*

All fruit has a better colour and flavour if preserved in syrup, but water may be used if desired.

From 4 to 8 oz. sugar to 1 pint of water is the usual strength of syrup. Dessert pears are better if bottled in a syrup with 12 oz. sugar to 1 pint water.

The amount of syrup needed varies with the kind of fruit. An approximate quantity is $\frac{1}{2}$ pint of syrup to 1 lb. fruit, but it is better to prepare a little extra, and if left over it can be used for stewing fruit or making a fresh fruit salad.

To make the syrup.

1. Weigh the sugar.
2. Measure the water. Put half the water in a pan, add the sugar.

F

3. Dissolve slowly, then bring to the boil. Remove from the heat.
4. Add the rest of the measured water. This cools the syrup more quickly. If boiling syrup is to be used make the syrup from all the water at once.
5. When boiling syrup is needed cover the saucepan with a lid to prevent evaporation.
6. If the syrup is not quite clear strain through butter-muslin.

(2) *The Jars.*

1. Wash the jars, lids, and clips or screw bands very thoroughly in hot soapy water.
2. Rinse carefully in clean cold water.
3. Leave the jars upside-down to drain. Do not dry with a cloth.
4. Leave the lids and clips or screw bands on a board ready for use.
5. Put the rubber bands to steep in a basin of warm water until required. Rubber bands should not be used if perished or cracked.

(3) *The Fruit.*

Fruit for bottling should be fresh, firm, and without blemishes. The fruit is usually described as firm-ripe.

1. Prepare the fruit, top and tail, remove stalks, leaves, and calyx.
2. Wash carefully, using cold water. Drain in a colander.
3. Pick out any bruised or damaged fruit; this can often be used for pies or for serving at once. If possible divide the fruit into even sizes so that all the small fruit can be bottled together. This is called grading the fruit.
4. Pack the fruit carefully into the jars. Wet jars help the fruit to slide in more easily. Fruit should be packed as tightly as possible; the handle of a wooden spoon is useful for reaching the bottom of the jar.

5. When half full stand the jar on a folded cloth and shake up and down a little to help the fruit to settle, then fill to the top with more fruit. Special methods of packing are given with the instructions for particular fruits.

To Sterilize, using the Water-bath Method

SPECIAL EQUIPMENT NEEDED

1. The equipment described on p. 150.
2. A large pan or preserving-pan.
3. A wire or wooden rack or a ring of double corrugated cardboard to fit the bottom of the pan.
4. A lid to keep in the heat and steam—a wire cooling-tray and a cloth is suitable.

(See photograph on p. 151.)

Method.

1. Follow the general instructions for syrup, jars, and fruit.
2. Estimate the number of jars to be filled, and calculate the amount of syrup required (see p. 151.)
3. Make the syrup and leave to cool.
4. Prepare the fruit according to kind, and pack tightly into the jars.
5. Stand the jars in turn on a plate, and fill to overflowing with the cool syrup. Use the spilled syrup from the plate.
6. Give the jars a quick twist round to remove air bubbles, cover with the rubber band, lid, and clip or screw band. If a screw band is used screw up tightly, and then unscrew for half a turn to allow for expansion. The clip acts as a spring and allows for expansion automatically.
7. Half fill the large pan or preserving-pan with cold water. Fit in the double ring of corrugated cardboard or a rack. Place on the stove where a gentle heat can be maintained.
8. Stand the bottles of fruit on the cardboard in the pan. The jars must not touch each other.
9. The water should cover the jars completely, but if they are

too tall allow the water to come as far up as possible, without making the pan too full.

10. Cover with a lid or wire cooling-tray and a cloth.
11. Turn on the heat and adjust very low. The water must heat very slowly to allow the heat to penetrate to the fruit in the middle without overcooking the fruit on the outside.

TIME TO ALLOW FOR STERILIZING

1. In all cases allow 1½ hours for the water to reach just below simmering point. The water must never be allowed to boil.
2. If a thermometer is used follow the temperatures and times given in the table below.
3. If no thermometer is used the water should become hot and steamy after 1½ hours' gentle heating. The water should be moving quietly, but not bubbling.
4. Keep the water at the same heat for 10–20 minutes according to the fruit.

Fruit	Temperature after 1½ hours	Time to keep at the temperature
Apricots		
Damsons		
Gooseberries	165° F.	10 minutes
Plums		
Raspberries		
Rhubarb		
Closely packed blackcurrants		20 minutes
Pears	190° F.	20 minutes
Tomatoes		25 minutes

To finish.

1. When the water has been kept at the temperature for the required time turn out the heat.
2. The pan of water with the jars is too heavy to lift, therefore ladle out sufficient water to expose the jars half-way down.
   Stand a wooden board on a firm surface as near as possible to the stove.
3. Use a cloth and lift out the jars one at a time on to the board.
4. Screw the metal bands up tightly at once.

5. Prevent sudden draughts, cover with a cloth if necessary, and leave to cool without disturbing for 12 hours.
6. When quite cold remove the clips or screw bands. Test the the seal of the jar by lifting the jar by the lid. The seal, or vacuum, should be strong enough to keep the lid in position.
7. Wash the clips or screw bands, dry in a warm place. When dry rub a little vaseline on the inside of the screw bands and replace loosely on the jars or store carefully. The clips may also be rubbed with vaseline and stored. Clips are better not replaced on the jars so that the spring of the metal is not stretched for long periods.
8. Label the jars clearly with the date, name of fruit, and whether preserved in syrup or water. Stick the labels on straight.
9. Store bottled fruit in a cool, dry, dark place.

Note.
   If the bottles are not sealed when tested the whole process should be repeated or the contents used at once.

To Sterilize, using the Oven Method

SPECIAL EQUIPMENT NEEDED

1. The equipment described on p. 150.
2. A cool oven.
3. A covering for the oven shelves to protect the glass jars. Cardboard, an old wooden board, or an asbestos mat may be used.
      The covering should be large enough for the jars to stand on, but should allow the warm air to circulate freely in the oven.

Method.
   1. Follow the general instructions for syrup, jars, and fruit.
   2. Arrange the shelves low in the oven, and wide enough apart to take the jars. Prepare the cardboard or other covering for the shelves, and set the oven to very low— Regulo 1 or 250° F.

3. Prepare the fruit according to kind, and pack tightly into the jars.

4. Without adding any syrup cover the jars with the lids only and stand in the oven on the protective covering. The jars should not touch each other.

5. Allow 1 to 1½ hours. Solid or closely packed fruits, e.g. apricots or blackcurrants, need longer than soft or loosely packed ones, e.g. gooseberries or plums.

6. While the fruit is cooking calculate the amount of syrup needed. Make the syrup in a pan with a lip, and keep it hot. Cover with a lid to prevent evaporation.

7. Prepare the rubber bands, clips or screw bands, and a wooden board.

8. Care must be taken when opening the oven door to prevent sudden draughts which might cause the glass jar to crack and splinter. Keep the face well away from the oven when opening the door at first. Accidents are only likely to happen if the oven becomes too hot.

9. When ready the fruit should be cooked right through, but must be quite whole. Pay special attention to the fruit in the middle of the jar when deciding whether it is ready.

10. Use an oven cloth and lift out one jar at a time. Stand it on a wooden board, fill at once with boiling syrup, fit on the rubber band and hot lid, and finally fasten on the clip or screw band. Screw up the band tightly at once.

11. When all the jars are covered put together on a board and leave to cool without disturbing for 12 hours.

12. When quite cold follow the instructions Nos. 6 to 9 on p. 155 for finishing.

Note.

1. If water is used instead of syrup have a kettle of boiling water ready for filling the jars.

2. If the oven has been too hot the fruit will be over-cooked and will shrink in the jars. If this happens use one jar of fruit to fill up the rest.

3. Fruits such as pears and tomatoes which need higher temperatures should only be preserved by the water-bath method.

Special Points for Particular Fruits

BLACKCURRANTS

1. Bottle firm unbroken fruit.
2. Remove stems, but leave the brown heads.
3. Blackcurrants are better bottled in a strong syrup—8 oz. sugar to 1 pint water.

GOOSEBERRIES

1. Bottle when green and firm.
2. Top and tail close to the berry so that there is a small cut surface which allows the syrup to penetrate.

PEARS

1. Bottle using the water-bath method.
2. Use ripe dessert pears.
3. If cooking pears are used stew them first in syrup until just tender, and then pack unto the jars and use the same syrup to cover.
4. Before peeling pears prepare a large bowl of cold salt water. Allow 1 tablespoonful salt to 2 quarts water. When the pears are peeled put them into the salt water at once to keep them a good colour. Put a plate over the pears to keep them well pressed down in the salt water.
5. Pears are usually bottled in halves. Peel whole, then cut in half, and scoop out the core with a teaspoon.
6. When all the pears are prepared drain in a colander, and rinse away the salt in fresh cold water. Pack into the jars, and cover at once with the cold syrup.
    Another method is to pack the jars one at a time, then rinse each jar in cold water, empty, and cover with the cold syrup.
7. Most people like pears bottled in a very strong syrup, 12 oz. sugar to 1 pint water.

PLUMS

1. Bottle plums when at the firm ripe stage.
2. Victoria plums are a good variety to bottle.
3. Choose small plums, so that as many as possible can be packed into the jars.
4. Plums may be halved, stoned, and packed cut side down. This makes a more solid pack, and the bottles should be sterilized at the higher temperature, as for pears. (See the table, p. 154.)

RASPBERRIES

1. Raspberries must be bottled as soon as possible after picking or buying.
2. Because raspberries pack so closely it is better to use a strong syrup—8 oz. sugar to 1 pint water.

RHUBARB

1. Bottle young tender rhubarb.
2. The rhubarb is easier to pack into the jars if cut into 2-inch lengths.

TO BOTTLE TOMATOES

There are several methods of bottling tomatoes. The following method is a popular one, and the tomatoes are useful for serving as a vegetable or in soup or stew.

TOMATOES IN THEIR OWN LIQUID

1. Use firm but ripe tomatoes.
2. Prepare a pan of boiling water and a bowl of cold water.
3. Use a draining spoon or fish-slice, and dip each tomato in the boiling water. Count five, then lift out and plunge into the bowl of cold water.
4. Skin the tomatoes and cut into halves or quarters if large.
5. Mix together 1 rounded teaspoon each of salt and sugar to 2 lb. tomatoes.

6. Pack the tomatoes cut side down in the prepared jars and sprinkle the salt and sugar mixture between each layer. Pack the jars tightly to the top.

7. Cover with rubber band, lid, and clip or screw band. Stand on the corrugated cardboard in the deep pan of cold water. (See instructions for bottling, using the water-bath method, p. 153.)

8. See the table for temperature and time on p. 154.

9. Finish as described on p. 155, Nos. 6 to 9.

Note.

Owing to the solid pack of the tomatoes approximately 2 lb. tomatoes are required to fill a 1-lb. preserving jar.

APPLE PULP

Apple pulp is a very useful preserve. It can be served as stewed fruit or makes a ready-to-serve apple sauce.

Apple pulp is a good way of preserving windfall cooking apples which may be too bruised to keep.

1. Prepare preserving-jars, rubber bands, lids, and clips or screw bands as for bottled fruit. Then put the jars and lids to warm.

2. Prepare a deep pan or preserving-pan with a rack or cardboard to fit the bottom.

3. Half fill the pan with water and put on to heat slowly.

4. If possible choose apples of the same variety so that they make the same kind of pulp. Allow approximately 4 lb. apples to fill a 1-lb. preserving-jar.

5. Wash, peel, and core the apples. Cut out bruised or damaged parts. Stew in very little water, with just sufficient sugar to sweeten lightly, until a thick pulp is formed.

6. Stand the hot jars on a wooden board, fill to the top with hot pulp, cover with the rubber band, lid, and clip or screw band as quickly as possible. Unscrew the metal bands half a turn.

7. Use a cloth to put the jars one at a time into the pan of hot

*F

water. Stand firmly on the cardboard or rack. The jars should not touch each other. The water should cover or come to the neck of the jars.

8. Cover with a lid. Bring to the boil, and boil gently for 10 minutes.

9. Turn off the heat; if the pan is very full ladle a little water out with a cup to expose the tops of the jars. Use a cloth and lift out the jars one at a time on to a wooden board. Screw down the metal bands at once.

10. Leave to cool undisturbed for 12 hours, then follow the instruction for testing and finishing, Nos. 6 to 9, on p. 155.

BOTTLED VEGETABLES

Young vegetables may be bottled if a suitable pressure cooker is available. They make a change in the winter months when fresh vegetables are scarce.

Vegetables cannot be bottled at ordinary temperatures as for fruit. This is because the vegetables do not contain sufficient acid to destroy the harmful bacteria.

Use a reliable pressure cooker with a gauge to measure the pressure. Follow the instructions for bottling vegetables given with the pressure cooker. This is very important, as the pressure may cause the glass jars to shatter if they are cooled too suddenly, or if the cooker is opened too soon.

VEGETABLES SUITABLE FOR BOTTLING

Small new potatoes.	Green peas.	Small broad beans.
Young carrots.	Runner beans.	

Chutney

Chutney is a smooth thick mixture of cooked acid fruits, onions, dried fruits, spices, salt, sugar, and vinegar. Many different flavours can be developed, and recipes are often adapted to suit particular family requirements.

GENERAL RULES FOR MAKING CHUTNEY

1. Never make very large quantities, particularly when trying out a new recipe.
2. Chutney is not usually sieved.   The ingredients are prepared so that they break down completely, e.g. skin tomatoes, peel and core apples.   Large quantities of fruit and onions are usually minced.
3. The consistency should be like very thick cream; there should be no liquid separate from the other ingredients when a spoon is drawn through the chutney in the pan.
4. Typical chutney jars are square.   These are attractive, but can be wasteful in use.   Ordinary jam jars may be used if properly covered.
5. The vinegar causes unprotected metal covers to rust. Chutney will become dry, due to evaporation, if covered with ordinary jam covers.

SUGGESTIONS FOR COVERING

1. Metal tops lined with special shiny yellow paper, which is resistant to vinegar.
2. Synthetic preserving skin tied on when hot (see photograph on p. 137).   This may be washed and used again in following years.
3. The jar may be covered with greaseproof paper, and then tied down with a circle of clean white cotton material which has been dipped in melted paraffin wax.
4. Several layers of brown paper.

APPLE CHUTNEY

3 lb. apples.	1½ lb. brown sugar.
2 pt. vinegar.	1 oz. ground ginger.
1 lb. onion or shallots.	1 oz. salt.
¼ lb. raisins.	½ a level teasp. Cayenne pepper.

To make.

1. Choose a large pan or preserving-pan. Wash, peel, core, and cut up the apples; put at once into the pan and cover with the vinegar.
2. Peel and chop the onions finely. Wash and chop the raisins. Add to the apples.
3. Add the rest of the ingredients and put over the heat. Heat slowly until the sugar has dissolved, bring to the boil, then simmer slowly, stirring occasionally until the chutney is thick and smooth. This will take 1 to 1½ hours.
4. Prepare clean dry jars and put to warm. Prepare the covers.
5. When the chutney is the correct consistency (see General Rules, p. 161) stand the hot jars on a board, lift the chutney on to a pan-stand, and use a jug over a plate for filling the jars as for filling jam jars.
6. Fill the jars to within ½ inch of the top. Scrape out the pan, jug, and plate to fill the last jar. Clean the sides and rims of the jars.
7. If using synthetic skin cover whilst hot. Do not trim the skin, then it may be used again. Use soft string for tying. Other covers are put on when the chutney is cold.
8. When cold label neatly with the date and kind of chutney.
9. Store in a cool dry place, and allow to mature for a few months before using.

TOMATO CHUTNEY

2 lb. ripe tomatoes.	1 pt. vinegar.
1 lb. apples.	1 level teasp. ground ginger.
½ lb. onions or shallots.	1 level teasp. mixed spice.
½ lb. sultanas or seedless raisins.	½ a level teasp. Cayenne pepper.
1 lb. brown sugar.	1 level tablesp. salt.

To make.

1. Prepare a pan of boiling water and a bowl of cold water. Dip the tomatoes one at a time into the boiling water

for 5 seconds, then plunge them into the cold water. Peel
and cut up.

2. Peel, core, and chop the apples. Peel and chop the onions
finely. Wash the sultanas.

3. Put all the ingredients together in a preserving-pan. Cook
slowly until the sugar has dissolved, then simmer gently
1 to 1½ hours until thick and smooth.

4. Finish as for Apple Chutney, p. 162, Nos. 4 to 8.

Note.

Many chutneys may be made in the same way.
Other popular fruits to use are gooseberries, plums, rhubarb, and green
tomatoes.

Pickles

Pickled vegetables and fruits make very appetizing extras to
cold-meat dinners and bread-and-cheese suppers. The pre-
servative used in pickles is usually spiced vinegar. A good
pickle should be crisp.

PICKLED ONIONS OR SHALLOTS

4 lb. small onions or shallots.   1 qt. spiced vinegar to cover.
½ lb. salt.

To spice ⎧ A small piece stick cinnamon.
the ⎨ 6 cloves. 5 pieces mace.
vinegar ⎩ 3 bay leaves. 1 dessertsp. whole spice.

To prepare.

1. Prepare the onions or shallots. Use a stainless knife, cut off
the ends cleanly, peel and pack in layers in a mixing-bowl
with the salt. Use dry crushed cooking salt, and allow
4 oz. salt to each 2 lb. shallots or onions. Cover and
leave to stand for 24 hours.

2. Prepare the spiced vinegar. Tie the spices in a small piece
of muslin. Put the spice bag and vinegar in a pan and
bring to the boil. Remove from the heat, pour into a

jug or a basin. When the vinegar is quite cold remove the spices.

3. Spiced vinegar may be prepared several days before required. Store in a spare vinegar bottle.

4. After 24 hours pack the shallots into jars. Pack tightly, but leave the neck of the jar free.

5. Cover with the cold spiced vinegar. The vinegar must be about ½ inch above the shallots to allow for evaporation during storage.

6. Cover the jars with synthetic skin or metal tops, protected with vinegar resisting paper. Clean the jars. Label and store carefully.

7. Pickled shallots should not be used for at least two months.

PICCALILLI

This is a mixture of vegetables in a mustard sauce.

1 lb. small onions or shallots.	1 small cauliflower.
1 lb. marrow.	½ cucumber.
½ lb. runner or french beans.	

Standard Brine

3 to 4 pt. water.	½ lb. salt.

Sauce

3 oz. flour.	½ oz. turmeric powder.
2 oz. mustard.	1 qt. vinegar.

To make.

1. Choose very fresh crisp vegetables. Peel and cut up into chunky pieces of a suitable size for eating. Onions are more popular left whole.

2. Put the salt in a large mixing-bowl, add the water, stir until dissolved, then add the prepared vegetables. Cover and leave to steep for 24 hours.

3. Next day drain the vegetables in a colander. Prepare the jars and put to warm.

4. Blend the flour, mustard, and turmeric with a little of the cold vinegar in a large pan. Add the rest of the vinegar and stir over gentle heat until it thickens and boils.

5. Add the drained vegetables, and cook slowly for 3 to 4 minutes until warmed through. The vegetables must not soften.

6. Pack the vegetables into the hot jars, distributing the kinds of vegetables evenly through the jars. Pour in sufficient mustard sauce to cover the vegetables.

7. Clean the sides and rims of the jars. Cover with synthetic skin or metal tops with vinegar papers. Label and store for a few weeks before using.

TOMATO SAUCE

Sauces or ketchups being sieved and concentrated are more extravagant to make, but are very delicious to eat. Tomato sauce is particularly good served with fried foods. Sauces keep better if sterilized after bottling.

6 lb. ripe tomatoes.	½ level teasp. ground ginger.
½ lb. granulated sugar.	½ level teasp. mixed spice.
¾ oz. salt.	½ level teasp. ground mace.
½ pt. vinegar.	Pinch Cayenne pepper.

To fill approximately 5 sauce bottles.

If white vinegar is used the sauce is a brighter red.

To make.

1. Wash the tomatoes, cut up into quarters, and put in a large saucepan.

2. Cook slowly until the juice begins to flow, then simmer until the tomatoes are broken up. Cook without a lid to allow some of the liquid to evaporate.

3. Place a hair or nylon sieve over a mixing-bowl and, using a wooden spoon, rub the tomato pulp through the sieve, leaving the seeds and skins.

4. Put the dry bottles and a jug to warm. Rinse the saucepan, return the sieved tomato pulp, the sugar, spices, salt, pepper, and vinegar.

5. Cook slowly until the sugar has dissolved, and then simmer

without a lid until the pulp is thick and will coat the back of the spoon.

6. While the sauce is reducing to the correct consistency prepare a pan of boiling water for sterilizing. This is similar to the method for sterilizing Apple Pulp (p. 159).

7. Prepare a large pan half full of hot water. Cut a double ring of corrugated cardboard to fit the bottom.

8. When the sauce is the correct consistency lift the pan on to a pan-stand. Pour the sauce into the warmed jug and fill the hot bottles to within 1 inch of the top.

9. Clean the edges and rims of the bottles, and cover at once with synthetic skin. Tie firmly with soft white string. Pull the pleats of the skin down under the string, so that the top is stretched tightly. Stand the bottles a little apart on the false bottom in the pan of hot water. The water should reach to the neck of the bottles.

10. Bring the water to the boil and boil gently for 15 minutes.

11. Turn off the heat. Ladle out sufficient water to expose the tops of the bottles and lift out on to a wooden surface.

12. When cool the skin should be drawn inwards. Label neatly, and keep for several weeks before using.

Salting

The salting of meat and fish is one of the oldest methods of preserving food for the winter. Vegetables and fruits are more commonly salted at home, e.g. runner beans and nuts.

TO SALT NUTS

Hazel nuts and filberts are the most suitable.

1. Choose clean dry nuts, remove the green hulls, and examine the nuts. Take out any black or withered nuts, and any which have small holes in the shells: these will contain no kernel.

2. Pack the nuts in a jar: a 7-lb. stone jar makes a useful jar for storing nuts. Sprinkle a little dry salt between each layer.

3. Cover the jar with brown paper and use as required.

4. Chopped nuts are useful for decorating biscuits or short-bread, and for flavouring small cakes.

TO SALT RUNNER BEANS OR FRENCH BEANS

3 lb. beans.   1 lb. cooking salt.

It is better to use the whole of a jar of beans once it has been opened, therefore choose jars of a suitable size for the family. Glass or stone jam jars are suitable for salting beans.

To prepare.

1. Choose very fresh young beans. Wash, dry, and remove the strings.

2. Leave small French beans whole. Slice runner beans as for cooking.

3. Crush the salt on a piece of paper.

4. Pack the salt and beans in layers in the jars, beginning and ending with salt. Press the beans well down. Fill each jar to the top.

5. Cover with lids or several layers of brown paper. Do not allow metal lids to touch the salt or they will corrode.

6. After a few days the beans shrink in the jars. Remove the covers, fill up from a spare jar, and finish with a fresh layer of salt. Re-cover.

7. Store in a cool, dry place.

8. When using wash the beans very thoroughly to remove the salt and cook in boiling water without salt.

Drying

Drying is also a very old method of preserving. In sunny climates fruit and vegetables are dried in the sun. Herbs are simple to dry and are useful in the winter-time when fresh herbs are scarce. Smaller quantities of dried herbs are used as the flavour is concentrated.

TO DRY THYME AND OTHER SMALL-LEAVED HERBS

1. Pick fresh, young thyme. For the best flavour pick the herbs early in the day, and when they are dry.
2. Wash carefully, shake and tie in bundles. Cover the bundles in muslin or a paper bag to protect from the dust. Hang to dry near a stove for several days or until the leaves are crisp.
3. When crisp strip off the leaves on to a clean sheet of kitchen paper. Crush the leaves finely, sift through a gravy strainer to keep back pieces of stalk.
4. Store in small jars with a very tight lid. Label clearly.
5. It is important to keep well covered so that no flavour is lost and no moisture allowed to enter.

TO DRY SAGE AND OTHER LARGE-LEAVED HERBS

1. Pick young, fresh, dry leaves.
2. Strip the leaves from the stalks and tie in a piece of muslin.
3. Prepare a pan of boiling water.
4. Dip the leaves in the muslin into the boiling water for 1 minute.
5. Shake the leaves dry and spread on a baking-tray covered with paper.
6. Dry in a very cool oven, 120° F., or in a warm place above the stove. Dry 1 to 3 hours or until the leaves are crisp and will crumble easily.
7. Cool the leaves, crush finely, sieve, and store in small jars. Cover tightly and label.

TO DRY PARSLEY

1. Pick fresh, young parsley. Wash and dry well in a cloth.
2. When dry spread on a baking-tray on paper, and put in a very hot oven for 1 minute. This helps to fix the green colour. Do not brown the parsley.
3. Finish drying the parsley in a cool oven, as for sage, until it is crisp and will crumble.
4. Crush finely, sieve and store in small jars with a tight lid. Label neatly.

GLOSSARY

Au gratin. This is used to describe a dish which is coated with sauce and sprinkled with breadcrumbs, or breadcrumbs and grated cheese. The dish is then browned in the oven or under the grill, e.g. cauliflower *au gratin.*

Bake blind. To bake a pastry case without a filling.

Baste. To ladle hot fat over meat, eggs, etc., during cooking in order to keep the surface moist.

Blanch. To put into cold water, bring to the boil, and drain off this water.

Blend. To mix smoothly. This term is often used to indicate mixing together a powder with a little cold liquid.

Bouquet garni. A bunch of herbs tied in muslin and used to flavour soups and stews.

Cake mixtures :

1. A plain cake mixture is a mixture in which the proportion of fat to flour is half or less. In this case the fat is incorporated by rubbing-in.

2. A rich cake mixture is a mixture in which the proportion of fat to flour is more than half. In this case the margarine and sugar are creamed together.

Consistency. This is the feel and look of a mixture before baking.

1. A stiff consistency is usually obtained by mixing with a fork; the fork should stand upright if placed in the finished mixture.

2. A mixture of a dropping consistency is one which will drop from a wooden spoon when shaken.

3. A mixture of a soft dropping consistency is one which will drop from an unshaken wooden spoon if it is held above the bowl. It should do so whilst three is counted.

4. A coating consistency is the term usually applied to a sauce used for covering the surface of dishes. When tested the sauce should be thick enough to cover the back of the wooden spoon smoothly, and should leave no ridges as it drips back on to the sauce in the pan.

To cream.

1. The term is used in making rich cake mixtures, and means to beat together the margarine and sugar until the mixture is pale and light like whipped cream.

2. A second use is in making yeast mixtures, when the term means to mix together the yeast and a little sugar until liquefied.

Dredge. To sprinkle lightly on a surface.

Garnish. To make a dish attractive by decorating, e.g. with sprigs of parsley, lemon butterflies, etc.

Panada. A thick binding sauce.

Purée. A thick sieved mixture, e.g. fruit purée for fruit fool; vegetable purée for soups.

Réchauffé. Reheated.

Roux. Equal quantities of fat and flour cooked together to form the basis of a sauce.

Rubbing-in. This is a method of incorporating fat with flour. The fat is first cut in pieces in the flour, then both are lifted and sprinkled with the thumb and finger-tips until the mixture has the appearance of breadcrumbs.

Sauté. To fry lightly.

Simmer. To keep a liquid just at boiling point. Only slight bubbling and movement of the liquid is seen. An asbestos mat placed between a pan and the heat is often useful to keep the heat sufficiently well controlled.

Sponge. The process in dough-making during which the carbon dioxide gas is produced from the yeast with the sugar and warm liquid. After 15 to 20 minutes the mixture bubbles and froths and resembles a sponge in appearance.

HANDY WEIGHTS AND MEASURES

1. Teaspoons, tablespoons, and tea-cups are the best things in which to measure ingredients if no scales are available.

2. If a teaspoonful is mentioned in a recipe a rounded spoonful is meant—as much above as in the bowl of the spoon. Half a teaspoonful would therefore be a level spoonful.

3. A rounded tablespoonful=2 level tablespoonfuls.

4. A heaped tablespoonful=3 level tablespoonfuls.

Note.

As spoons vary in size it is better to compile a list of your own. The following list is accurate when using an ordinary tablespoon. If a basting or large metal spoon is used read rounded instead of heaped, and level instead of rounded.

SPOONFULS

1 heaped tablespoonful flour or other fine grain	=1 oz.
1 rounded tablespoonful sugar, currants, and other similar ingredients	=1 oz.
1 rounded tablespoonful unmelted treacle	=2 oz.

TEACUPFULS

1 teacupful flour =4 oz.

1 teacupful sugar=6 oz.

Remember. New blocks and packets may be marked into portions.

LIQUIDS

1 teacup brimful =$\frac{1}{3}$ pint

8 tablespoonfuls =$\frac{1}{4}$ pint

1 gill =$\frac{1}{4}$ pint

173

CHART OF OVEN HEATS

Very Moderate	Moderate	Fairly Hot	Hot	Very hot
250° F. Regulo 1–2	300° F. 3–4	350°–400° F. 5–6	400°–450° F. 7–8	450°–500° F. 9

Note.

As ovens vary, after successful baking always make a note against the recipe indicating the setting or temperature of the oven and the other details of baking. This is useful for future reference.

INDEX

INDEX

177